The Effective DRE:
A Theology Series

That All May Be One:
Ecumenism

BY BR. JEFFREY GROS, F.S.C.

TOM WALTERS
SERIES EDITOR

NATIONAL CONFERENCE FOR
CATECHETICAL LEADERSHIP

 Loyola Press

**NATIONAL CONFERENCE FOR
CATECHETICAL LEADERSHIP**

3021 Fourth Street, N.E.
Washington, D.C. 20017-1102
1-202-636-3826

 **Loyola Press**

3441 North Ashland Avenue
Chicago, Illinois 60657
1-800-621-1008

This booklet is dedicated to
Brother Norman McCarthy, F.S.C.
A Lasallian catechist for the long haul

Nihil Obstat: Rev. Daniel J. Mahan, S.T.B., S.T.L.
   Censor Librorum
Imprimatur: Rev. Msgr. Joseph F. Schaedel
   Vicar General/Moderator of the Curia
Given at Indianapolis, Indiana, on December 21, 1999
Feast of St. Peter Canisius

The *nihil obstat* and *imprimatur* are official declarations that a book is free of doctrinal and moral error. No implication is contained herein that those who have granted the nihil obstat and imprimatur agree with the content, opinions, or statements expressed.

Acknowledgments:
The Scripture quotations contained herein are from the New Revised Standard Version Bible, Catholic edition,©1993 and 1989 by the Division of Christian Education of the National Council of the Churches of Christ in the U.S.A. Used by permission. All rights reserved.

Excerpts from the English translation of *Rite of Christian Initiation of Adults* ©1985, International Committee on English in the Liturgy, Inc. All rights reserved.

Excerpts from *Vatican Council II, Volume1, Revised Edition: The Conciliar and Post Conciliar Documents* edited by Austin Flannery, O.P. copyright © 1998, Costello Publishing Company, Inc., Northport, NY are used by permission of the publisher, all rights reserved. No part of these excerpts may be reproduced, stored in a retrieval system or transmitted in any form or by any means electronic, mechanical, photo-copying, recording or otherwise, without express permission of Costello Publishing Company.

Excerpts from *Baptism, Eucharist and Ministry* ©1983 WCC Publications, and *On the Way to Fuller Koinonia* ©1994 WCC Publications are used by permission of the World Council of Churches, Geneva, Switzerland. All rights reserved.

Excerpts from the *General Directory for Catechesis* ©1997 United States Catholic Conference, Inc.—Libreria Editrice Vaticana. Used with permission. All rights reserved.

Excerpts from *The Ecumenical Dimension in the Formation of Those Engaged in Pastoral Work* ©Libreria Editrice Vaticana, 00120 Città del Vaticano. Used with permission. All rights reserved.

ISBN: 0-8294-1491-6

00   01   02   03   04   5   4   3   2   1   Printed in Canada

Table of Contents

About This Series

The Effective DRE: A Theology Series has been developed by the National Conference for Catechetical Leadership (NCCL) to provide directors of religious education (DREs) and those preparing to become DREs with an introductory and orderly understanding and interpretation of the truths of revelation. As in the earlier series, **The Effective DRE: A Skills Development Series**, we use the term DRE as broadly as possible and intend it to refer to anyone involved in or planning to become involved in a leadership capacity in a parish religious education program. And, also like the earlier series, these booklets, though addressed specifically to DREs, can be of assistance to all parish catechetical leaders, regardless of their title or the scope of their job description.

Each booklet was written to assist DREs in meeting the theological requirements specified in the *National Certification Standards for Professional Parish Directors of Religious Education*, a document developed by the NCCL and approved by the United States Catholic Conference Commission on Certification and Accreditation. The series covers the following topics: Scripture, Sacramental Theology, Church History, Ecclesiology, Christology, Morality, Ecumenism, Mary and the Saints, and Theological Reflection.

Each booklet is written with the intent of helping DREs gain access to the Catholic tradition in a way that allows them to apply it to their lives and their catechetical ministry. It is our hope that these booklets will serve not only as a personal resource for self-study but also as a resource in formal diocesan and parish training programs for catechetical leaders/DREs. The reflection questions at the end of each chapter lend themselves not only to personal reflection but group discussion as well.

In addition, the authors have drawn extensively from both the *Catechism of the Catholic Church* and the recently published *General Directory for Catechesis*. This has resulted in a series that is both informative and up-to-date.

Like the earlier series, this series is designed to serve as a resource to DREs in their efforts to foster the growth of faith in those whom they serve.

Tom Walters
Series Editor

Introduction

This booklet introduces the DRE's task in helping catechists and parishes understand and play their role in building unity among Christians. For Catholics, the goal of the visible unity of the Church is central to Catholic identity. As Pope John Paul II reminds us, ". . . it is absolutely clear that ecumenism, the movement promoting Christian Unity, is not just some sort of 'appendix' which is added to the Church's traditional activity. Rather, ecumenism is an organic part of her life and work, and consequently must pervade all that she is and does; it must be like the fruit borne by a healthy and flourishing tree which grows to its full stature" (*Ut Unum Sint*, #20).

The *National Certification Standards for Professional Parish Directors of Religious Education* (*NCS*) specifically proposes three important dimensions of our catechesis:
1) an "understanding of the Catholic faith tradition in relation to other Christian traditions"; 2) the "religious beliefs, gifts, values, and traditions commonly shared by the different Catholic Churches and other Christian communities"; 3) "the significant ecclesiological renewal confirmed by Vatican Council II" (#520.06, #520.15, #520.17).

During the last thirty years, catechists—and DREs in particular—have carried a unique and challenging role. While they have been charged primarily with transmitting the Christian faith and a deep love for the Church, they have also been confronted with the additional challenge of providing the catechesis for introducing the reforms of the Second Vatican Council.

For example, while catechists teach the permanent
Christian faith regarding Christ's real presence in the
Eucharist, they also help adults and students understand
liturgy in their own language, the new prayers of the
Mass, and the expanded use of Scripture in the lectionary.
With each new sacramental revision, development in the
Church's social teaching, and new expression of lay leader-
ship, educators are challenged to bring adults and young
people deeper into the mystery of Christ.

Some may raise the question: Shouldn't Catholic formation take place before ecumenical elements are introduced?
The answer is *no*. Catholic formation essentially *includes*
ecumenical formation as central to one's identity as a
Catholic. Roman Catholicism cannot be understood properly without knowing its ecumenical zeal and program. To
delay the ecumenical component in the formation of
Catholic identity would be like allowing people to only go
to Latin Masses until they reach a certain age, or allowing
racist and anti-Semitic attitudes to flourish until people are
"mature" enough for Catholic social teaching. To teach
Christ and his Catholic Church is to teach Christ's will for
unity and the Church's involvement in this pilgrimage.

The ecumenical pilgrimage has been particularly challenging. To the extent we are open to the Council's call to
conversion and to deepening the bonds of unity among
Christians, Catholics are continually renewing the Church
and deepening relationships with fellow Christians.
Responsiveness to Christ's prayer and following the call to
full communion among the churches provide new experiences to incorporate into our catechesis and new opportunities for learning about the Catholic tradition.

The *General Directory for Catechesis* (*GDC*) makes clear
that educational work is integral to evangelization. This
new evangelization is an evangelization "new in ardor,

methods and expression" (Pope John Paul II, Haiti, March 1983). The new evangelization includes elements such as:

1) awakening to full sacramental participation and lay leadership among nominal and dormant Catholics;

2) initiating an authentic inculturation and dialogue of cultures;

3) engendering conversion to the social teaching of the Church as well as to personal, sacramental transformation in Christ;

4) stimulating ecumenical commitment: "The new evangelization is the order of the day . . . The task of evangelization involves moving toward each other and moving together as Christians, and it must begin from within; evangelization and unity, evangelization and ecumenism are indissolubly linked with each other. . . . Because the question of the new evangelization is very close to my heart, as bishop of Rome, I consider overcoming the divisions of Christianity 'one of the pastoral priorities'" (Pope John Paul II, Germany, July 1996);

5) building upon the strengths of the true disciples of Christ who have gone before us, learning from and asking forgiveness for sins and errors of the past, and moving into a purer and more inclusive promotion of the Gospel;

6) receiving all the elements of renewal in the Council: biblical, religious liberty, liturgical, collegiality, ecumenical, co-responsibility,

lay leadership, witness for peace and justice, the universal call to holiness, etc.;

7) articulating the Gospel and our Catholic heritage in the face of a variety of new challenges: secular, other religious streams, reliance on culture as a substitute for personal faith, privatization and individualizing of religion, and the like (see *GDC*, #26-28, #58c, #276-277).

In ecumenical catechesis, method and content, experience and information, spiritual formation, and cognitive content are essentially complementary to one another. They all need to be considered as the DRE and the catechist deepen their ability to serve their students. "It remains easy to fall into a 'content-method' dualism, with resultant reductionism to one or other extreme; with regard to the pedagogical dimension, the requisite theological discernment has not always been exercised (cf. *Catechesi tradendae*, #58)" (*GDC*, #30).

Since embarking on the road toward the unity of the churches in 1964, there has been a rich harvest of internal Catholic developments. This has included deepened relationships on the parish, national, and universal level with fellow Christians.

In this booklet we will:

• note the context of catechetical work in light of the Church's teaching and American culture;

• focus on the methods and content of Catholic formation on the ecumenical horizon;

• look briefly at the churches with which we relate, and note the level of relationships;

• introduce the implications of the dialogues for catechesis in various areas;

- survey the concerns important for sacramental preparation;

- provide suggestions for developing experiences of ecumenical mission;

- enumerate resources that can be helpful in formation for unity.

This volume will help with *NCS*, #520.01-21 in particular.[1]

This brief beginning should assist the DRE who is commencing the ecumenical pilgrimage. It can be a resource for those who have been immersed in ecumenical ministry in the decades since the Second Vatican Council. It is an exciting journey, and these notes are only a start and stimulus.

---

[1] It also will contribute to developments in #510.03, 07, 10, 13; 531.02–03; 531.042; 531.06; 532.101–102; 532.201–2032; 532.301, 303–306; 532.4021, 4022; 533.01–031, 08; 534.01, 03; 535.02, 041, 042, 06; and 539.032, 04, 07–101 according to the content of each of these criteria and their ecumenical significance, as will be noted throughout the book.

Abbreviations

ARC 1	*Called to Full Unity: Documents on Anglican-Roman Catholic Relations, 1966-1983*
ARC 2	*Common Witness to the Gospel: Anglican-Roman Catholic Documents, 1983-1995*
BEM	*Baptism, Eucharist and Ministry* of the World Council of Churches
BU	*Building Unity*
BWA	Baptist World Alliance
CCC	*Catechism of the Catholic Church*
DAPN	*Directory for the Application of Principles and Norms on Ecumenism*
DC	*Deepening Communion*
EFPW	*Ecumenical Formation of Pastoral Workers*
ERCDOM	*Evangelical Roman Catholic Dialogue on Mission*
FO	*Documentary History of Faith and Order: 1963-1993*
FU	*Facing Unity*
GA	*Growth in Agreement*
GC	*Growing Consensus*
GDC	*General Directory for Catechesis*
JD	*Joint Declaration on the Doctrine of Justification* (Lutheran-Catholic)

JWG	Joint Working Group, World Council and Catholic Church
LWF	Lutheran World Federation
NAE	National Association of Evangelicals
NCCB	National Conference of Catholic Bishops
NCS	*National Certification Standards for Professional Parish Directors of Religious Education*
NCC	National Council of Churches of Christ in the USA
OO	*Oriental Orthodox-Roman Catholic Pastoral Relationships and Interchurch Marriages*
Ox	*The Quest for Unity*
PCPCU	Pontifical Council for Promoting Christian Unity
RCIA	Rite of Christian Initiation for Adults
SBC	Southern Baptist Convention
UCC	United Church of Christ
UMC	United Methodist Church
USCC	United States Catholic Conference
UUS	*Ut Unum Sint* Encyclical: *That They May Be One*
WARC	World Alliance of Reformed Churches
WCC	World Council of Churches
WCC93	*On the Way to Fuller Koinonia*, Thomas F. Best and Günther Gassman, eds. Geneva: WCC, 1994.
WEF	World Evangelical Fellowship

1 Teaching for Christian Unity

I n 1965, when the Second Vatican Council was in full swing, I took a group of young brothers in formation to worship with a local Pentecostal Church of God congregation at the bottom of the hill from our novitiate in Glencoe, Missouri.

Accustomed to a prefabricated Latin worship, as we were in those days, we were initially unnerved by the animation of the worship. When the congregation accepted our return invitation to worship with us during the week of prayer for Christian unity, they were wide-eyed at the crucifix and statues in our chapel. (We decided to worship in the music room with piano rather than organ.) Many of the young brothers continued to visit this Pentecostal church and made friends there as part of the spiritual discipline of their novitiate.

One could not imagine in 1965 that by 1970 there would be a full-blown Catholic charismatic movement, that by 1975 there would be a scholarly society with full Catholic and Pentecostal participation, that by 1980 there would be a productive dialogue between the Vatican and Pentecostals, and that by 1998 the Vatican/Pentecostal dialogue would publish a common statement entitled *Evangelization, Proselytism and Common Witness.*

Hopefully, those young men who experienced an early conversion to interest in fellow Christians developed into catechists who welcome the development of relationships and understandings between Pentecostals and Catholics.

Undoubtedly, they have encouraged others to follow a similar pilgrimage. This conversion and subsequent development is a great resource for their catechesis.

In this chapter we will look at 1) the ecumenical horizon of our catechesis; 2) some specific dimensions of inculturation in our ecumenical catechesis; and 3) the resources the Church provides to help us as educators in enabling our catechesis.

THE HORIZON OF OUR CATECHESIS

"Christ the Lord founded one Church and one Church only" (*Unitatis redintegratio*, #1). Thus it is God's will that the Christian churches be united. Our one Baptism into Christ is the foundation for communion among Christians. At the Holy Spirit's prompting, the Catholic Church and many Christian communities are striving to achieve that unity which is Christ's gift to the Church. This is the blessing and the challenge of the ecumenical movement.

Those involved in this catechetical task are challenged to ". . . assume an 'ecumenical dimension' everywhere" (*GDC*, #197, quoting *Catechesi tradendae*, #32). This means that, while engendering a love for Christ and a loyalty and affection for the Church, catechists are also called—as Pope John Paul II reminds us—to awaken a zeal for the unity of the Church. The catechists' role is to touch the hearts of students so that they are awakened to a zeal for the unity of the churches, and to engender in the students a desire to understand other churches. The implications of this understanding will be the ability to work with fellow Christians. Your catechists will create a receptivity to the steps that will promote the reconciling of our churches and faith in God's will for the unity of Christians.

This entails the *conversion* of church leadership and of catechists. Conversion, in fact, is central to all ecumenical efforts. Your catechists will need to see the vision of unity. Like the novices described above, they will need to be awakened to the vision of Christian unity and must come to an understanding of Catholic ecumenical principles. It will be important for them to understand the churches with which we relate and to develop the skills to serve the Church's ecumenical mission (see *NCS*, #510.03, .05; #520.11; *GDC*, #29, #53–57).

What's more, DREs must acquire ecumenical experience, an ecumenical spirituality, and sufficient knowledge of ecumenical developments to lead catechists and to help them provide a context for students in following Christ on this ecumenical pilgrimage. The theological basis for Catholic involvement in the ecumenical movement was developed in the Second Vatican Council and was further explored in the extraordinary Synod of 1985. Finally, it was codified in the *Catechism of the Catholic Church (CCC)* and *The Directory for the Application of Principles and Norms on Ecumenism (DAPN)*.

The word *ecumenical* comes from the Greek word meaning the "whole inhabited earth." It was first used by the Christians in the early Church to designate universality, or the whole Christian community worldwide—thus *ecumenical* councils. Since the last century, it has been used to designate the call for the universal unity of the Christian Church, especially in overcoming the divisions of East and West and of the Reformation of the sixteenth century.

For both catechists and students, it is important to distinguish between *interfaith* and *ecumenical*. *Interfaith* designates mutual understanding and collaboration with the world's religions outside Christianity. *Ecumenical* refers to the collaboration of Christians in prayer and witness and to their search for full reconciliation of our churches in Christ.

The *theology of the Church*, articulated by the Catholic Church and now current in ecumenical conversations, is that of communion (*koinonia*). It is grounded in the communion of Father, Son, and Holy Spirit, and in the communion between the baptized and the Trinity in Christ's saving death and resurrection. Catholics believe in the real, but imperfect, communion among all baptized Christians and in the call of all Christian churches to full communion in common faith, sacramental life, and witness. Everyone catechized in the Catholic faith will need to experience conversion toward this zeal for unity as central to Catholic identity. They will need to embrace the goal of full communion as the horizon of their hopes for the Church (see *NCS*, #520.17; *GDC*, #78–79).

THE U.S. CULTURAL SITUATION AND THE CHURCHES' QUEST FOR UNITY

As the *GDC* notes in its discussion of evangelization and catechesis, sensitivity to culture and *inculturation* are major priorities in the educational project. Some look at America as a secular environment. Studies show, however, that rather than being secular—in comparison with Europe, for example—it is a religiously diverse and pluralistic environment (see *GDC*, #21, #58–59, #109–113, #202 ff.).

Ecumenism is not about compromise or selling out to a lowest common denominator. Rather, it is a *serious commitment* to one's own understanding of religious identity. It calls for collaboration in love and service with fellow Christians with whom there is not yet full agreement and for the common search for unity based on the Gospel foundation of truth.

There are several aspects of American culture that are challenging to the task of building the unity of the Church. First, all the churches are struggling against the religious illiteracy and anti-intellectualism that dominate American life. The media, advertising, and the manipulation of truth in public and political life create both a skeptical and superficial approach to truth. Thus the task falls to DREs to help catechists develop skills to gain the attention of students. Religious education should help find commitment among the variety of options available in the modern world. Part of the catechetical task is to help develop loyalty and trust in the Church and its teaching. This challenge is not uniquely Catholic, of course; it is shared by our ecumenical partners. Common approaches in developing religious literacy, loyalty, and understanding are shared catechetical priorities.

Second, the pluralism of the U.S. religious situation fosters two tendencies: sectarianism and denominationalism (see *NCS*, #533.08; #535.06; *GDC*, #193). Both are foreign to a Catholic understanding of the Church and to the ecumenical vision shared among churches.

A *sect* is a group that defines itself over against those outside of it. It considers its saving truth the only truth and does not see God's saving work outside its borders. Catholicism has never considered itself a sect. Rather, it has always acknowledged the Orthodox to be true churches even if we are not yet in full communion. Catholicism is centered in Christ and his revelation; it is not non-Orthodox or non-Protestant (see *GDC*, #22). Catholics define themselves in positive terms, centered in Christ and recognizing their relationships with Orthodox and Protestant Christians.

Since the Second Vatican Council, Catholics have acknowledged the element of truth wherever it is to be found. They acknowledge the ecclesial reality within the churches of the Reformation that truly mediate God's grace in Jesus Christ to their members. The bishops at the Council decided to say that the one, true Church *subsists in* the Catholic Church, rather than asserting that the one, true Church *is* the Catholic Church.

A *denomination*, on the other hand, is a Christian body that believes itself to be a part of the Body of Christ, named (de-nominated) in a particular tradition. In such an understanding, one church community is equal to another. Visible unity is to be hoped for, but it is not a necessary part of the biblical understanding of the Church. This position easily leads to indifferentism about the true nature of the Church. As Catholics, we call one another the names others use of themselves. Therefore, we can call ecclesial communities *churches* even when we do not yet understand them to possess all we feel the Gospel demands for being the true *Church*.

Like the Orthodox, Lutherans, Anglicans, Baptists, and others, however, Catholics recognize some elements of Scripture and tradition that are grounded in the Gospel truth and are essential for the *Church*. Of course, we do not yet agree with all of these churches on what these essential elements are. This position contrasts with a "denominational" sense of toleration that Catholics have called *indifferentism*. Such a position diminishes the concern for truth and even the concern for ecumenical unity. While the bishops of the Council put aside the identification of the one, true Church with Catholicism, it affirmed that the true Church *subsists in* the Catholic Church.

Catechetically, it is a challenge to avoid these two tendencies in American Christian culture. It is important to form Catholics who are ecumenically open, committed to the core of the Catholic faith, and patient and urgent about the ecumenical journey together.

In preparing catechists, it is important for DREs to attend to the ecumenically *diverse religious contexts* within which we work. Ecumenism will be significant in isolated, urban ethnic contexts. In these situations, exposure to other Christians, their worship, and their faith may occur rarely and possibly only in our catechetical context. For situations where they are a minority, ecumenical formation will be essential if Catholics are to know fellow Christians with whom they live, how to relate to them, and what gifts the Catholic Church brings to the ecumenical movement (see *GDC*, #167–170).

A third aspect of American culture that is challenging to the task of building the unity of the Church is the fact that in specific ethnic communities, ecumenical catechesis will take on appropriate cultural forms. We will give only two examples here, but parallels within Eastern European, Irish, Southern-Evangelical, upper Midwest-Lutheran, and other cultural contexts can be developed as appropriate.

In the Hispanic communities, for example, new arrivals often do not have the experience of pluralism and the habit of living with fellow Christians, as do those who have lived with and related to other churches for generations. As a result, they may find Pentecostal and other evangelical Christians more hospitable and providing more Christian outreach than their Catholic parishes. These new arrivals will need to be welcomed, given a strong grounding in their Catholic identity, and helped in understanding the variety of Christian groups (see Peter Casarella, Raúl Gómez, *El Cuerpo de Cristo: The Hispanic Presence in the U.S. Catholic Church*, Crossroads Publishing).

African American communities offer another example. In nurturing African American Catholic ecumenism, sensitivity to the history of exclusion will be essential. The African American community is often characterized by the predominance of Protestant culture, where ministers have an important role in community and political life. In this community, ecumenical priority is given to common witness against racism and for justice.

We must take into account the sad history of Catholic schools being centers of proselytism of fellow Christians from these African American Protestant Churches. Before the Council, Christians were encouraged to leave their churches to join the Catholic Church. The Council, however, recognizes the saving character of other Christian churches and moves with them on the pilgrimage toward visible unity as churches. The Catholic Church is in dialogue with the African American Methodist, Baptist, and Pentecostal churches through the National Council of Churches of Christ in the USA (NCC) and in other ecumenical contexts.

Today, Catholic schools nurture the faith of their students within their own communities. The ecumenical task is one of reconciling churches and supporting one another. At this point, spirituality and social justice will characterize African American ecumenism, more so than theological or sacramental questions. When there are young people in our catechetical programs whose parents go to these churches, it will be particularly important to have the opportunity to know the African American minister and for that person to feel welcome in the Catholic community. It will be particularly important for catechesis in Anglo communities to provide black Protestant worship and dialogue experiences (see William Watley, *Singing the Lord's Song in a Strange Land*, World Council of Churches).

INSTITUTIONS OF THE ECUMENICAL MOVEMENT

In Chapter 6 we discuss the way parishes and dioceses are structured to help the catechetical work in promoting Christian unity. At this point, however, it may be useful to note some of the institutional structures provided for promoting unity among Christians. At the time of the preparation of the Second Vatican Council (1959), Pope John XXIII founded a Secretariat for Promoting Christian

Unity. This secretariat provided important leadership in the Council, not only with the non-Catholic observers and the ecumenical documents, but also with the theological formulations on the Church, Religious Liberty, Divine Revelation, the Church in the Modern World, and the like. In 1989, the secretariat was renamed the Pontifical Council for Promoting Christian Unity (PCPCU). It provides the leadership for the Catholic Church worldwide, serving the bishops and the Holy Father, sponsoring dialogues with other churches, and collaborating with other elements in the Roman Curia by helping them implement the ecumenical part of their work for the Church.

In many states and cities around the country there are local ministerial associations, conferences, or councils of churches where common witness, community service, prayer, and dialogue occur on a regular basis. On a national level there is the National Council of Churches (NCC), to which thirty-four Orthodox, Protestant, and Anglican churches belong. The Catholic Church collaborates in many programs of the NCC and is a full member of its Faith and Order Commission.

In 1948, a World Council of Churches (WCC) was formed, including over three hundred Orthodox, Anglican, and Protestant churches from around the globe. The purpose of the WCC is to call the churches to full visible unity in one faith, one eucharistic fellowship that the world may believe. The Catholic Church is a full member of its Faith and Order Commission and provides some staff to its Geneva office, but is not a member. There is Catholic collaboration in almost every element of the WCC.

The annual Week of Prayer for Christian Unity, developed internationally by the Holy See and the WCC, and in the United States by the National Council of Churches in Christ in collaboration with the National Conference of

Catholic Bishops (NCCB), is usually celebrated in January. It provides an annual opportunity for prayer, dialogue, and sharing among all Christians at least annually.

RESOURCES FROM THE MAGISTERIUM

DREs are fortunate to have a rich harvest of materials from which to draw on in their own formation and that of their catechists. In this section we note some of these documents and their use. Unless otherwise noted, these are available from the United States Catholic Conference (USCC). (See *NCS*, #531.02, #532.102, #535.02.)

Ecumenical Formation of Pastoral Workers, 1998 *(EFPW)*: This brief document is important reading for DREs in preparing the training of catechists in collaboration with diocesan ecumenical offices. It suggests a workshop or course early in the catechists' formation so that they can bring a view of the Church, as enunciated by the Second Vatican Council, to all their teaching. The *EFPW* provides details for this course and suggests how all catechist preparation can be permeated by the ecumenical vision. It also provides ideas for more specialized instruction. This document will inform much of this booklet.

General Directory for Catechesis, 1997 *(GDC)*: This directory provides specific sections on the ecumenical dimension of catechesis (#61, #86, #133, #172, #196, #197, #198). However, the emphasis on catechesis in the context of evangelization, inculturation, and liturgical life reinforces the importance of the ecumenical dimension of these elements in catechetical formation. DREs will want to study and implement the *EFPW* and the *GDC* together.

Ut Unum Sint, 1995: Pope John Paul II outlines where the Catholic Church has come since the Council, where the Church must go, and some of his own experiences and enthusiasm. This is a suitable text for catechists' retreat and for personal prayer and reflection. Its tone is enthusiastic and upbeat.

Directory for the Application of Principles and Norms on Ecumenism, 1995 (*DAPN*): This directory should be in every parish library and catechetical resource center. Under one cover, it synthesizes all the ecumenical principles of the Catholic Church promulgated since the Council. It includes chapters on the theological basis for Catholic involvement in the ecumenical movement, organization of the Church in service to unity, ecumenical formation, spiritual and sacramental ecumenism, and collaboration and dialogue. Chapter three on formation will be particularly important for catechesis in connection with *EFPW*. Chapter four provides the basis for the ecumenical dimension of sacramental catechesis, as we will note below in our Chapter 4. This directory brings Catholic ecumenism up to date with Canon Law (1983, 1991).

The *Catechism of the Catholic Church*, 1992 (*CCC*): Released in 1992, this now familiar resource provides a compendium from which much catechetical preparation and resources are drawn. It reiterates the conciliar vision on ecumenism (#815–855). It also articulates the doctrinal bases on which our agreements with other Christians are based and clarifies our differences.

The *CCC* is to be interpreted and implemented in the light of the subsequent magisterial contributions noted above. Likewise, if the results of the ecumenical dialogues are "to become a common heritage" (*UUS*, #80), as Pope John Paul II suggests, educators will need to provide resources for teaching and programs for catechists that relate these agreements among the Christian churches to the doctrinal elements of catechesis (see *GDC*, #119 ff). Chapter 5 notes some places where the ecumenical dialogues and the *CCC* can be used together.

Ecumenical Formation: Ecumenical Reflections and Suggestions, 1993: This study document of the Joint Working Group between the Roman Catholic Church and the WCC is not a product of the magisterium. However, it provides important advice useful to DREs. It can be a useful tool in working with fellow Christian educators from other traditions in formulating ecumenical programs for catechists. It discusses the ecumenical imperative, the process of exploration and learning, community pedagogy, ecumenical spirituality, the instruments of communication, and common witness (published in *EFPW* and *DC*).

In addition to the documents from the Church proper, there are doctrinal and pastoral resources that have been produced by officially sponsored dialogues with other churches and in councils of churches. These are gradually finding their way into volumes that should be in catechetical centers, diocesan and Catholic school libraries, and larger parishes.

There is not yet a synthesis of this material for catechetical use or for inclusion in teachers' guides. However, these dialogue results are an important resource in implementing the *EFPW*, the *GDC*, and the *CCC*. It will be important for DREs to know, with the help of the diocesan ecumenical officer, what is relevant for the catechetical work and the formation of parish catechists.

From the USCC: the Orthodox Dialogues: *The Quest for Unity (Ox)*; the Oriental Orthodox Dialogue: *Oriental Orthodox-Roman Catholic Pastoral Relationships and Interchurch Marriages (OO)*; the Anglican Dialogues: *Called to Full Unity: Documents on Anglican-Roman Catholic Relations, 1966–1983 (ARC 1)*, and *Common Witness to the Gospel: Anglican Roman Catholic Documents, 1983–1995 (ARC 2)*.

From Paulist Press: International Dialogues: *Growth in Agreement (GA)* and *Deepening Communion (DC)*; U.S. Dialogues: *Building Unity (BU)*, *Growing Consensus (GC)*. From the World Council: *Documentary History of Faith and Order: 1963–1993 (FO)* and *On the Way to Fuller Koinonia (WCC93)*.

While there are many more documentary resources, these are the basics. If DREs read *EFPW*, the *DAPN* in the context of the *GDC* and the *CCC*, and know where to find the other resources as needed, they have a tremendous reservoir for supporting the parish and catechists in this important ministry. Other resources are noted at the end of this booklet, including a summary *Introduction to Ecumenism*. This can be important background reading for those just beginning to learn about Catholic ecumenism.

SUMMARY

DREs may be challenged because the ecumenical dimension of catechist formation is such a daunting task. I remember when we began a new ecumenical commission in a new diocese in the early 1970s. The members of the commission, including the DRE who was representing the religious education board and the catechetical community, felt they did not know enough. Our response then was that there were no second-generation catechists who were formed ecumenists. We had to start somewhere, and we did.

We are lucky to have more resources today. We still have the challenge, however, to start somewhere. Some of us continue leadership with thirty years of ecumenical experience. Others are just beginning this pilgrimage. It is God's journey, so we do not judge our usefulness in his service by our ability and knowledge, but by the challenge of ignorance out in front of us.

If we need deeper conversion, more knowledge, and wider experience, then we have the hunger for the ecumenical movement that will serve us as DREs. This will provide the motivation to stimulate and inform catechists and students in their understanding of and quest for unity.

FOR REFLECTION

1. What was your first experience of faith sharing with other Christians? Which churches in your community do you know best? Which ones do you know least?

2. What areas of the Church's teaching about unity have been the most surprising and challenging for you? Where do you feel you need to do more study?

3. What challenges do you find to teaching ecumenism among your catechists and students? How do you experience Catholic attitudes toward Church unity as different from other Christians, or from the culture at large?

2 The Churches with Which Catholics Relate

When I was living in Good Shepherd parish in north Manhattan, I went to the Spanish Mass one Sunday morning in August to find Paulist Father Paul Rospond preaching on the Gospel text about Peter (Matthew 16:13–23). As you will recall, this text includes Peter's confession of belief in Christ's divinity, the promise of the "keys," and Christ's rebuke of Peter as "Satan."

Father Paul's homily was on the ambivalent role of Peter—and of his papal successors—as both foundation stone of faith and stumbling block toward unity. He quoted extensively, in Spanish, from agreed Lutheran-Catholic statements on papal primacy and infallibility. He adapted his preaching to the audience, most of whom did not have a high school education. However, he made clear the importance of the pope among the bishops of the Church. He emphasized the Holy Father's ecumenical service and the open discussion of the papacy among Christians.

He went on further to distinguish between our Lutheran and other ecumenical colleagues, and the Pentecostal storefront churches in the neighborhood—those people who might ring our Catholic doorbells to invite us to evangelical Protestant services. This good preacher was able to articulate, in the context of the Gospel reading, both Catholic affirmations and some of the ecumenical progress that has been made. He was able to clarify, in a direct and uncomplicated manner, the distinction between different churches. He explained the importance of different, but positive relationships.

In this chapter we will explore the "religious beliefs, gifts, values, and traditions commonly shared by the different Catholic churches and other Christian communities," so that we might "develop programs that would create openness among members of the parish community in their interaction with persons of other [Christian] traditions" (*NCS*, #520.15).

The concrete Christian community, and its particular ecumenical makeup, "becomes a point of concrete reference for the faith journey of individuals. This happens when the community is proposed as a source, *locus* and means of catechesis" (*GDC*, #158). This means that as Catholics learn about particular churches, their history, their relationship to us, and their spiritual life, they are learning about what God is doing in that community. They also learn how their own spiritual and ecclesial life is enriched by the Holy Spirit's presence in these fellow Christians and the common calling toward unity.

The best way for DREs to introduce catechists to other churches in the community is by inviting teachers or clergy persons from those churches to speak to the catechists. These guests can share copies of the catechetical material they use in training their own young people and membership candidates. They can be most helpful in explaining what Catholic students should know about the different churches in their community.

DREs can ask the diocesan director of ecumenism to come or send a representative to team up with a member of the other church in explaining where the dialogue is with that particular church, in the diocese and around the world. In some parishes and dioceses there are covenant relationships with particular congregations or denominations. DREs can help the catechists make these relationships part of the prayer life and catechetical program in a special way.

The Catholic Church has formal dialogues with churches of both East and West. Among the Eastern churches are the Assyrian, Eastern, and Oriental Orthodox churches. There are also dialogues with the Polish National Catholic Church, Anglicans (Episcopalians), Lutherans, Methodists, Reformed, Presbyterian, United Church of Christ (UCC), Disciples of Christ, Southern Baptists, and Pentecostals. The Church relates to a wide range of other churches through the Faith and Order Commissions of the World and National Council of Churches to which the Catholic Church has belonged since 1968. More is said about dialogues with these churches in Chapters 4, 5, and 6. In this chapter we briefly review the churches and Catholic relationships to them.

THE EASTERN CHURCHES

Western Catholics need to know of the variety of Eastern Churches in communion with Rome. These used to be spoken of as "rites." Since the Eastern Code of Canon Law, 1991, they are called "churches *sui juris*"(with their own legal tradition) which have their own synodical governance, their own proper spirituality, law, liturgy, and theology (USCC, *The Eastern Christian Churches*).

While these relationships are not properly ecumenical, since Catholics of both Latin and Eastern traditions are in full communion, catechetical programs need to "foster an understanding and appreciation of the churches, in addition to the Latin Church, that make up the Catholic Church" (*NCS*, #520.16).

Appreciation of the history and the attendance at the liturgy of these churches are important parts of our catechesis. DREs will need to help catechists recognize the tensions with both Latin Catholics, with whom they are in full communion, and with the Orthodox, whose traditions they share. Again, students and catechists can learn about these non-Latin Catholics by visiting them and hearing directly from their teachers and clergy.

Knowledge of national background and ethnicity are important factors in understanding the Eastern Churches, Catholic and Orthodox. Each of these churches has a particular cultural history that is a gift to its liturgical, spiritual, and ethical tradition, but can also be a burden that isolates the community from other Christians (see *NCS*, #531.06).

The Assyrian Church of the East and the Chaldean Catholic Church are of the same tradition and developed in the Persian Empire beyond the borders of the Roman Empire. The Oriental Orthodox churches were in Africa, Asia Minor, and Armenia, on the borders of the Roman world.

While *Oriental* and *Eastern* mean the same thing in English, they are used, in referring to the Orthodox, to distinguish those churches that have been separated from both Eastern Orthodoxy and Rome since the Council of Chalcedon (451 A.D.)—the *Oriental Orthodox*. Rome and Constantinople separated as Latin, Greek, and Slavic cultures began to diverge during the first centuries of Christianity, culminating in the Great Schism of 1054. These Eastern churches are called *Eastern* or *Byzantine* Orthodox.

Orthodox means "of the correct faith," so Catholics claim to be orthodox in faith as well. Likewise, the word *Catholic* in the title of the Catholic Church means "universal." Therefore, all the Orthodox churches and many of the Reformation churches claim catholicity and profess faith in the catholicity of the Church and their church in the Nicene Creed. *Roman* Catholic is sometimes used as the title of the Catholic Church, the churches in commu-

nion with the pope. There are a number of Eastern
churches in communion with Rome, which are not Roman
in their language, liturgy, piety, or theological tradition.
These *Eastern Catholic* churches are as Catholic as the
Roman Church.

In the present day, the language of "schismatic" and
"heretic" is seldom used by Western Christians, but the
differences of perception between West and East are no
less real and profound. The Eastern Orthodox consider
the Catholic Church to have left the united communion of
the first millennium. Catholics, however, claim that the
divisions of 1054 and thereafter were mere schisms that
did not affect the apostolic faith, sacramental life, and
Episcopal structures of the churches, East and West.

The Catholic Church recognizes the sacramental character of these "sister churches" and insists that any study of
the nature of the Church take full account of developments
of both East and West. Pope John Paul II continually
reminds Catholics that the Church must learn to breathe
again "with both lungs." The first thousand years of full
communion is a common resource for reform and renewal.

The East has been much less centralized than the West,
and has synods of bishops around the various patriarchs to
make decisions. Councils of the Church are seen to be the
highest authority. In the West, the Catholic Church has
come to rely increasingly on the ministry of unity provided by the pope, the bishop of Rome, in the second millennium of Christianity. The dialogue with each of these
three sister churches of the Eastern tradition is an important contribution to discerning the future God desires for
us together.

ASSYRIAN CHURCH OF THE EAST

At the Council of Ephesus (431 A.D.), the churches
attempted to resolve their differences in speaking of Mary

either as the mother only of the humanity of Jesus Christ, or as the mother of Jesus as both human and divine. To some, an unwillingness to speak of the "God bearer" (*theotokos*) appeared to question the full divinity of Christ; to others, the use of the title appeared to question Christ's full humanity. The Persian Church, with its patriarchate at Seleucia-Ctesiphon, called *Nestorian* by its critics, did not accept the Council and fell out of communion with the five apostolic patriarchates.

The Assyrian Church of the East, as it is now called, with centers in Iran, Iraq, and the United States, flourished throughout Asia and the Middle East during the Middle Ages. Today, the issue of Ephesus, on the nature of Mary as the mother of Jesus, human and divine, is being resolved. Pope John Paul II and Patriarch Mar Dinkha (See of his patriarchate in Chicago) signed a common declaration in 1994 to this end.

ORIENTAL ORTHODOX CHURCHES

The Council of Chalcedon (451 A.D.) dealt with emphases in Christology debated by the theological schools of Antioch and Alexandria. Following this Council, the issues continued to be debated for centuries, and several councils were called by the Byzantine emperors—in collaboration with the patriarchs of Constantinople and Rome—to heal the divisions and arrive at common formulations of the Christological faith.

As a result of these debates, however, about half of the patriarchate of Antioch (now the Syrian Orthodox Church) and most of the Church of Alexandria (now the Coptic Orthodox Church) separated from the patriarchs of Constantinople, Rome, and Jerusalem. The Armenians, Indian, Syrian, and Ethiopian churches shared these Christological views as well.

These churches are now called Oriental Orthodox, but in the past were often stigmatized as *Monophysite*, which means "one nature" in Christ. They in turn characterized the Latin and Byzantine churches as *Dyophysite*, which means "two natures" in Christ. In the present time, Christological agreements have emerged that have made common declarations possible between these churches and the Byzantine, Popes Paul VI and John Paul II, and some of the Reformation churches. Now we can both say that we believe Jesus Christ is truly human and truly divine, fully God and fully human.

In 1981, Pope John Paul II and Syrian Orthodox Patriarch Ignatius of Antioch published a common declaration, setting to rest differences on Christology and authorizing mutual eucharistic hospitality.

EASTERN (BYZANTINE) ORTHODOX CHURCHES

The Eastern Orthodox churches consider the West to have broken away from the common tradition. This view has factual support in the events of 1054 and 1204. In 1054, for example, the representative of the pope in Constantinople excommunicated the patriarch, who returned the insult. There was, however, no pope alive at the time! These condemnations were "assigned to oblivion" by Pope Paul VI and Patriarch Athenagoras (1964). Then, in 1204, the Fourth Crusade from the Western Christians took over Constantinople, desecrated the cathedral, and set up a Latin bishop. This sacrilege is not forgotten in Orthodox history.

Likewise, developments such as the addition of the phrase "and the Son" *(filioque)* to the common creed, papal centralization and infallibility, the Marian dogmas in Catholicism, and the ordination of women in Protestantism are seen as unilateral developments, moving away from the apostolic heritage.

Sacramental theology has also developed with different emphases. The Orthodox are not able to easily recognize the sacraments of the Catholic Church as being true sacraments. Catholics, however, are able to recognize the true nature of the sacraments of the Orthodox churches.

It is claimed that the first millennium recognized a basic unity between the churches. Ecumenical proposals exist that would remove the *filioque* phrase from the liturgies of various Western churches. Such a decision, of course, would depend on Orthodox ability to recognize the underlying theology as authentic.

In areas of liturgy, the use of leavened and unleavened bread has been considered divisive. Rebaptism, on occasion, has been practiced between the churches. There have been tensions over the evangelization of what are now eastern Europe and the Balkans. The claims of the patriarchate of Constantinople to be the new Rome and the claims of the patriarchate of Rome to a universal primacy that was more than one of honor have never been resolved and have often caused tensions.

Most historians of both East and West now recognize that the Fourth Crusade of 1204 was the final blow to unity and trust. The Byzantine Orthodox have never forgotten the sacrilegious cruelty of the Western "Christian" invaders, who sacked the cities and churches, replaced the canonical bishops with Latin prelates, and desecrated the holiest of sanctuaries.

In the United States most of the patriarchates have members: the Greeks and the Antiochean (Arabs), along with various Slavic groups. The Orthodox Church in America has various national constituents—Russian, Serbian, Ukrainian, etc.

The resistance of the Latin bishops in the early twentieth century to the agreements of some Eastern Catholics and the Holy See sent many of them back into communion with Orthodoxy. Therefore, both the historical tensions as well as the continuing tensions created by the U.S. Latin leadership must be taken into account. The dialogues with the Orthodox in the U.S. have been easier than international dialogue, especially after the fall of communism in 1989, when tensions in eastern Europe reemerged.

There are significant numbers of Eastern Orthodox in the U.S., and care needs to be taken to recognize the special relationship and delicate history involved. For example, preparation for Matrimony and Orthodox students in Catholic schools are particularly important concerns for DREs, since the Orthodox tend to have more stringent requirements than do Catholics. Also, Catholics are more open to sacramental sharing with the Eastern churches than are most of the Orthodox communities.

We now offer an overview of the Reformation churches and Catholic relationships with them. It will be important for DREs to provide catechists with resources that will help them move deeper into those relationships that are important in the particular parish and dioceses, and where their students have a parent in one of these churches.

CLASSICAL PROTESTANT AND ANGLICAN CHURCHES

Within the Latin Church of the West, a series of divisions developed that culminated in the Reformation of the sixteenth century. Some of the pre-Reformation divisions, such as those between rival popes in the fourteenth century, were healed, but not without a burden of distrust and cynicism concerning ecclesiastical institutions. Others, such as those with the Waldensians (excommunicated in 1183), Wycliffe (1330–1384), and the followers of the Bohemian reformer Jan Hus (c. 1372–1415) continued into the sixteenth century. They were eventually associated with Reformation churches in history, theology, and ecumenism. Waldensian and Moravian churches exist in the U.S., but they are small.

The context of the Reformation was complex and differed in the various parts of Europe. When teaching Catholic history, it is important to acknowledge that fault lies on both sides of the divisions. Catholics, in particular, approach history with a sense of repentance and a commitment to the healing of memories (see *UUS*, #2).

ANGLICANS AND LUTHERANS

In 1517, at the University of Wittenberg, Martin Luther (1483–1546) began to pose academic questions drawing on his pastoral experience about good works, especially the sale of indulgences. His studies led him to a passionate conviction of the importance of preaching God's unmerited justification by grace through faith. This, in turn, led him to question the emphasis placed in the Church of his day on human effort and merit in achieving salvation. He had no intention of creating a schism in the Church. He came to take more confrontational positions as the questions he raised were at first rejected. Many of the reforms in preaching the sales of indulgences that he advocated became part of the Council of Trent a half century later.

In 1518, at the initiative of his Augustinian superior, Luther was released from his vows. After 1521, when he stood up for his convictions before Emperor Charles V at Worms, he became an outlaw in the empire. His emphasis on the authority of Scripture in theology and the Church, the centrality of Christ, grace and faith over good works, and ecclesial and sacramental practices brought him into the center of tensions between Germanic forces for reform and the established ecclesiastical and civil authorities of pope and emperor.

The Reformation only hardened into a separation after the Augsburg Confession (1530), which was drafted as an irenic statement of the evangelical princes within the Catholic empire. It became the theological platform for the protesting princes and their theologians against the leadership of the Catholic Church.

These churches emphasize the priesthood of all believers, the role of the civil leaders in church life, the centrality of Scripture and proclamation in worship, the real presence of Christ in the Eucharist (simplified and celebrated in the vernacular), and above all the centrality of the Gospel teaching on justification.

Many of the Catholic practices—liturgical, spiritual, and artistic—were retained, including the episcopal structure of the Church where possible. The doctrinal tradition of the Church from the early councils remains central to a Lutheran sense of fidelity to the apostolic Church. Eventually, the Catholic Church was able to rectify some of the theological and ecclesiastical abuses of the day and to clarify its positions at the Council of Trent (1545–1563), after discussion with the Reformers had broken off.

In our own day, common ground has been found in regard to the doctrine of justification, the Eucharist, and many other divisive issues of the sixteenth century (see USCC, *The Lutheran-Catholic Quest for Visible Unity: Harvesting Thirty Years of Dialogue*).

It will be important for DREs to see that catechists present the Reformation and Catholic relations with Protestant churches in the light of the present state of dialogue (Chapter 5). Both DREs and catechists will want to teach agreements and differences as they exist now, and not the way they were formulated before Catholic entry into the ecumenical movement.

When Catholic history is taught in more detail, just as much attention needs to be given to ecumenical history

(1964 to the present) as might be given to a similar period in the sixteenth century (1517–1546). Catechists and students need to read the earlier history through the lens of present understanding of one another (see *EFPW,* #11).

In England the Reformation took a very different course. Originally, Henry VIII (reigned 1509–1547) was a staunch defender of the traditional faith and a persecutor of reformers. In order to obtain his divorce and ensure royal succession, however, he broke with Rome. As a result, both continental Protestant and continuing Catholic influences were in competition for the faith of the English people. Thereafter, the English Reformation remained a confluence of Reformation and Catholic elements, with many Anglicans claiming continuity with, and even return to, the situation that prevailed in the medieval period.

A short return to the papal obedience under Mary (1553–1558) was ended under her successor Elizabeth I (1558–1603). In 1559, the monarch was named supreme governor of the English Church in an ecclesiastical settlement that featured a moderate *Book of Common Prayer* (Anglican "Missal"), incorporating Catholic and Reformation elements, and an episcopal ecclesiastical order that claimed continuity in the apostolic succession. Since the Second Vatican Council, the Catholic Church has acknowledged a special relationship with the Anglican tradition.

The dialogue with the Holy See and the Anglican Communion—and in the U.S. with the Episcopal Church—has produced important agreements, pastoral proposals, and bases for mutual understanding (see *ARC 1* and *ARC 2*). Many dioceses and parishes have covenants with their local Catholic counterparts. Because of both agreements and continuing differences, common educational programs between DREs and Episcopalian Christian education directors is important, as well as opportunities for catechists to talk, study, and plan together.

The dialogues between Episcopalians and Lutherans are best known among Catholics. However, it will be important also to review the other Protestant churches, especially since the Methodist and Baptist communities are the largest churches in the United States.

REFORMED, METHODIST, AND DISCIPLES

The Presbyterian Church and other Reformed churches, such as the Reformed Church in America, the Christian Reformed Church (both are of Dutch background), and the United Church of Christ (UCC), owe their origins to the Swiss reform of John Calvin (1509–1564) which spread to Scotland, Holland, and England. The expression *Reformed* is used to distinguish the Calvinist tradition from Lutheran and other Reformation churches. The Congregationalists (now UCC) and Presbyterians have had a strong influence on American forms of decision making as well as wider cultural issues. The UCC is to be distinguished from the Churches of Christ; the latter are a nineteenth century American network of churches.

Calvin and Scottish reformer John Knox insisted on the full participation of the baptized in the governance of the Church. Thus, most Reformed churches have no bishops. Rather, there are both clergy and laity at every level of collegial decision making. It is useful for those preparing to work in parish councils or diocesan pastoral councils to visit a Presbyterian session or presbytery meeting with Presbyterian friends to see how lay involvement in collegial decision making can work.

Reformed churches are also sacramental, though their doctrine of the Eucharist has developed in a historically different and less universal direction than the Anglican and Lutheran traditions. Catholics have had important international dialogues with the Reformed churches, including dialogues on important issues of ethics (Chapter 6; see *GA, DC, BU,* and *GC*).

The Methodist churches (United Methodist and three African American churches: African Methodist Episcopal, African Methodist Episcopal Zion, and Christian Methodist Episcopal churches) are the largest family in the U.S. ecumenical movement. However, they are smaller internationally than Lutheran and Anglican communions. Their strong emphases on spirituality and social involvement make them the natural ecumenical partner for Catholics on the local level around the U.S. DREs will find their Methodist Christian education colleagues important collaborators in the catechetical ministry and helpful partners in finding service placements for those preparing for Confirmation.

Methodism was a revival movement within Anglicanism. John Wesley (1703–1791) found separation necessary at the time of the American Revolution. He was devoted to sacramental as well as biblical and evangelistic renewal, usually receiving Communion five times a week. While there is an office of bishop, they do not claim apostolic succession. Methodists are moving toward reconciliation with Anglican churches in the U.S. and various places around the world.

In 1969, the United Methodist Church revised its formula of faith to change those things that could be interpreted as against the Catholic Church, so they would no longer condemn Catholicism. Catholic dialogues with the United Methodist Church in the U.S. and the World Methodist Council have been extensive, but less focused than dialogues with the Anglicans and Lutherans (see *BU, GC, GA,* and *DC*). However, a common sense of mission, the gift of these two churches for organization, similar ecumenical commitment, and a uniform distribution throughout the country make these churches important ecumenical partners.

Thomas Campbell (1763–1854) and Barton Stone (1772–1844) attempted to begin an ecumenical movement. They developed congregations with open membership, possessing no creed but Christ and practicing weekly Eucharist and adult Baptism. From this movement emerged the Churches of Christ, the Christian Churches, and the Disciples of Christ. There has been an important Disciples Catholic Dialogue in this country and with the Holy See (see *BU* and *DC*). Disciples, like Methodists, are among the most ecumenically active churches in any community.

The Reformation also produced the Mennonite Church, which clings to a strong peace commitment, as do the Quakers (Religious Society of Friends) and the Church of the Brethren that emerged in later centuries. It will be important to find ways for these smaller churches and others in your community to explain themselves to the Catholic people. Parish social justice committees often find work with the peace churches an important dimension of their ecumenical program (see Peggy Shriver, *Having Gifts That Differ*, Friendship Press).

With the Eastern and Oriental Orthodox, the ecumenically oriented Anglican and Protestant churches created the National Council of Churches in 1950. Although the Catholic Church is not a member, there is close collaboration on a variety of ecumenical issues. The National Conference of Catholic Bishops is a full member of the NCC Faith and Order Commission. Many states and cities have conferences or councils of churches to provide a basis for ecumenical dialogue, common prayer, and witness to society. DREs can help catechists and students know about the ecumenical collaboration that goes on in the city and state councils of churches where they live.

In addition to Protestant and Orthodox churches that are committed to the ecumenical movement with the Catholic Church, there are many other Christian groups more or less open to collaboration, common witness, and dialogue, but that do not relate formally to other churches in ecumenical work. We will briefly survey these churches and Catholic relationships with them, where they exist.

EVANGELICAL AND PENTECOSTAL CHURCHES

All Christians consider themselves "evangelical" in the sense of being committed to the Gospel of Jesus Christ. In Europe, "Evangelical" is used as a name for the Lutheran churches to distinguish them from the Reformed, that is Calvinist, churches. In the United States, "evangelical" tends to designate conservative churches—Pentecostal, Baptist, Holiness, or Independent—that do not belong to councils of churches, have a history of polarization with the classical Protestant denominations, and have an aversion for Catholicism and Orthodoxy. However, there are many ecumenical spirits in the evangelical Protestant community.

Evangelicals form a loose movement of churches, most of which do not belong to the traditional ecumenical movement. They have a vast web of connections among themselves, including a National Association of Evangelicals and a World Evangelical Fellowship (WEF). They still have much mistrust of Catholicism; although their Christian seriousness, deep spiritual lives, concern about pro–life and family issues, and interchurch marriages have created important bridges, they do not see full communion with the Catholic Church and other Christians as their goal.

Sensitivity to and knowledge about these Christians in the local community—and outreach to them—are important. Above all, students need to know the difference between these churches and the churches to which Catholics are committed on the pilgrimage toward full communion.

Baptists' insistence on the separation of church and state, on baptizing only believing adults, on understanding Baptism and the Lord's Supper as ordinances rather than sacraments, and on private interpretation of the Scriptures set them apart from the earlier Reformation traditions. Baptists' emphasis on evangelism and congregational independence has contributed to their becoming the largest Protestant community in the United States today.

The American Baptists are ecumenically active. Other communities are not. The Holy See has had one round of dialogues with the Baptist World Alliance (see *DC*).

For over thirty years there has been a productive conversation with the Southern Baptist Convention, the largest U.S. denomination (see *BU*). Although this dialogue is not well known, it is an important resource for Catholics, especially in the South where this community is so large and active.

Among the Baptists and Methodists in the eighteenth and nineteenth centuries, numerous divisions emerged over race, slavery, and a variety of doctrinal emphases. As a result, there are three large African American Baptist groups (National Baptist Convention of America, Progressive National Baptist Convention, and National Baptist Convention, USA) and three large African American Methodist churches (African Methodist Episcopal, African Methodist Episcopal Zion, and Christian Methodist Episcopal) in the United States. These churches are evangelical in their faith, while active ecumenically in the councils of churches and in the quest for social justice (see *NCS*, #531.06).

There are, additionally, a cluster of Wesleyan movements that have developed into the Holiness churches, such as the Church of the Nazarene, the Wesleyan Church, the Free Methodists, and Church of God (Anderson, Indiana).

The nineteenth-century urgency about the second coming of Christ at the end of time produced a variety of movements which have developed into churches, the most prominent of these being the Seventh-Day Adventists.

After the turn of the century, a Pentecostal revival movement began. It is usually dated from a 1906 Azuza Street meeting in Los Angeles, California. This movement has developed into one of the fastest growing Christian communities in the late twentieth century.

Much of the theological impetus for this revival developed out of the Holiness movement and its Wesleyan emphasis on experience, the Holy Spirit, and a second work of grace. Speaking in tongues, faith healing, and baptism of the Holy Spirit are among the characteristics of this revival. It eventually gave rise to churches such as the Assemblies of God and Church of God in Christ. For twenty-five years there has been a Pentecostal Catholic dialogue with many U.S. participants (see *GA* and *GC*).

There is also an important Vatican dialogue with the World Evangelical Fellowship. A statement on *Evangelical Roman Catholic Dialogue on Mission* (*ERCDOM*) was published in the 1980s (see *DC*).

One may be surprised at how far relationships between Catholics and Evangelicals have developed, especially in local situations. This has occurred through the important leadership of individual priests and other church workers. Father Avery Dulles, S.J., suggests an interim strategy for developing informal ecumenical relationships:

1) Correct misleading stereotypes, in the interest of truth, justice, and Christian charity.

2) Be open to surprise in the authenticity of the Christian faith and practice of others.

3) Reach toward recognition of the holiness and resources for spirituality in all ecumenical partners.

4) Find ways of removing suspicion, fear, and resentment and to support one another spiritually by prayer, advice, and mutuality.

5) Develop respect for the religious freedom and integrity of others.

6) Pursue an ecumenism of mutual enrichment, learning to give and receive truth from one another without compromise.

7) Rejoice in the common Scripture, common prayer, and common hope of eternal life that already unites us.

8) Engage in joint witness and social action in areas where joint convictions are shared.

9) While we remain in separation, be open to growth in peace and patience. Only grace transcends the seemingly insuperable Christian divisions.

10) Continue to pray to Christ that we may all be one, a prayer that can only be realized by the power of the Holy Spirit.

SUMMARY

In the United States, cultural characteristics such as pluralism and a sense of individual initiative have developed into
an environment where a host of independent churches, of
various types, exists. These churches range from the storefront preacher of the urban neighborhood to the suburban
megachurches. This Christian diversity requires consider-
able ecumenical discernment for Catholic educators, especially those working with immigrant communities and
communities where Catholics may be the majority.

Although the Catholic Church is the largest religious
body in the U.S., some Catholics continue to think of
themselves as part of a minority since there are more people in the country who are not Catholic, unlike Latin
America or southern Europe. There is no Christian body,
however, that sees itself as a majority next to the enormous
number of Catholics. This places a certain ecumenical
leadership in Catholic hands, and a need for sensitivity
about Catholic numbers and power, which are greater
than any other religious community in the U.S.

This chapter noted the three varieties of Eastern
churches. We surveyed the spectrum of ecumenically oriented churches and indicated where there are dialogues
with Catholics. We discussed briefly evangelical churches
and Catholic relations with them, where such contacts are
possible.

Catechist formation can only begin a learning process
about these communities. DREs can collaborate with ecumenical colleagues and diocesan ecumenical leadership in
developing the ecumenical relationships that will enable
teachers to help their students enter into lifelong spiritual
learning and praying. Such a catechetical process will help
deepen the communion among the churches and to stimulate leadership in healing their differences.

FOR REFLECTION

1. Which are the predominant churches in your community? What is the Catholic Church's relationship to them? What is your parish's relationship to them? What do your students need to know to help them relate better to these churches?

2. How do the more ecumenically oriented churches in your community differ from the more closed churches? Is the Catholic Church an ecumenical leader in your community or does it need stimulation?

3. Which of the churches in the neighborhood are most comfortable in your Catholic community? Which are the most reticent? How can your parish be more hospitable and outgoing?

3 Elements of Catholic Ecumenical Formation

When I was DRE in St. Augustine's parish in the South Bronx in 1970, we wanted to devise a culturally sensitive Confirmation preparation program that would serve the Christian militancy of the young African American and Puerto Rican confirmands within a context of competition with the Black Panthers and Puerto Rican gangs.

We invited all the ministers who were related to the parish to be in the sanctuary when the bishop came for the celebration. We had worked with some of them as sponsors for the Confirmation service projects, like the Methodist soup kitchen. Others were members of the neighborhood organization with the Catholic clergy or were pastors of some of the non-Catholic parents. We did not know, exactly, if communion for them was possible. Of course, the Second Vatican Council had articulated the two principles: 1) the Eucharist is central in building up the unity of the Church and 2) the Eucharist is the sign of unity achieved among Christians. At that time, without clear guidelines, the DRE did not advise the pastor.

By 1973, the Holy See had issued guidelines authorizing the bishop to oversee questions of sacramental sharing. In 1983, the new Code of Canon Law, amplified in the

1993 ecumenical *DAPN*, authorized the Catholic minister to carry out this discernment in the light of diocesan guidelines. In the 1970s, also, Lutheran and Anglican agreements on the Eucharist emerged, followed by the WCC's *Baptism, Eucharist and Ministry* (*BEM*) text in 1982, and convergence statements with Methodists and Presbyterians in the 1980s. Today, DREs have many more resources than were available in the years immediately after the Council.

In Chapter 1, we noted the basis of Catholic commitments in the Christian faith and outlined the teaching of the magisterium calling for conversion and study. This chapter will focus on 1) the principle elements for an ecumenical approach; 2) the dimension of all formation if it is to be truly Catholic in its ecumenical vision; and 3) the elements to be included in the formation of DREs and catechists (see *EFPW*; *GDC*, #87; *DAPN* ch. 3).

This material will help DREs reflect on the "foundational elements of Vatican Council II" (*NCS*, #520.06) and understand "the uniqueness of the Catholic faith tradition in relation to other Christian traditions" (*NCS*, #520.17). It should assist DREs and catechists in helping "members of the parish community articulate Catholic beliefs and practices, especially the key elements of the Catholic faith" (*NCS*, #520.17).

THE ESSENTIALS OF ECUMENISM AND CATECHESIS

Prayer and worship are central to the ecumenical movement and to Catholic participation in it. DREs will want to help teachers develop a spiritual life, within their parishes and among their students, that is rooted in God's will for the unity of the churches in Christ. This means that DREs will need to show catechists how to provide experiences of prayer with other Christians, including prayer for other churches and for the unity of the Church. Such prayer will begin in the earliest stages of Christian development of both children and adults seeking to become Catholic. In order to help the catechists, DREs will want to order the Week of Prayer materials in due time and arrange for other Christians to participate with the catechists and their students in these prayers.

The Week of Prayer for Christian Unity is a privileged moment for prayer with other Christians and prayer for the unity of the Church. It is celebrated in most parishes and dioceses during the month of January. This is an opportune time for DREs to bring catechists and other adults together for spiritual reflection and study of the progress toward unity made during the past year. The diocesan ecumenical officers can be helpful in these efforts.

The pilgrimage toward full visible unity, and toward deepening bonds of communion in local parishes, calls for more than an annual prayer together, however. DREs can collaborate with parish liturgists and Christian educators from other churches to provide in-service programs for catechists, appropriate to the community, to go with the Week of Prayer celebration.

Serious civic events or neighborhood concerns also provide opportunities for the churches to produce prayers that can be used in all the churches on a given Sunday. When an event is planned or a concern is pressing in one congregation or church, it can be shared for the prayers of the faithful in the other churches. DREs can work with their parishes to provide such prayer opportunities to the catechists and help the catechists explain to their students the significance of this kind of ecumenical prayer.

When ecumenical breakthroughs are announced, like a new report from the Methodist dialogue or the Lutheran-Catholic *Joint Declaration on the Doctrine of Justification (JD)*, or an Episcopal delegation visits Rome, prayers of thanks-giving and a brief catechesis about the significance of the event can be planned.

Other ideas for sharing the spiritual lives of our church-es and working together on building up the spiritual unity of the churches include joint retreats with catechists and other Christian educators. DREs can invite ministers from other churches to provide ecumenical services and homi-lies for students or for diocesan catechetical congresses. These are good opportunities for the spiritual sharing that nourishes ecumenical prayer.

It is also important to have the experience of sharing the regular Sunday liturgy of other churches, even while full eucharistic communion is not yet possible. This gives teachers and students a chance to understand the spiritual-ity of fellow Christians and heightens the eagerness for the day when worship together can be fully shared. DREs can encourage catechists to make such arrangements, or they can open up the communication that will make such "field trips" possible.

Besides prayer and worship, the ecumenical experience of dialogue is also important. DREs themselves and their catechists should be provided opportunities to participate in such dialogue. When we would set up diocesan dia-logues with the various churches, I made sure that a DRE was among those around the table (see *NCS*, #531.03, .05; #533.01–031; #535.041, .042).

DREs, of course, don't need all the theological training of the theologians who write the documents. However, they do need to have a sense of how these agreements are reached so that they can help catechists teach their stu-dents about the truths central to these agreements (see *GDC*, #68, 143, 152).

Catechists should be encouraged to invite clergy and Christian educators of other churches into their classes.

DREs can help catechists do this or direct them to the diocesan ecumenical office that can help. This kind of Christian hospitality is an important element of the ecumenical mission of the Church. After all, the dialogue of truth has to be based on the dialogue of love.

DREs also need to find opportunities for catechists and students to feel at home in other churches, not only churches in their own neighborhood, but churches in other cultures and traditions as well, like Pentecostal or Orthodox. Experiences of common witness and service are integral to a holistic approach to catechesis today.

Encounters with other churches should not only stir Catholic students to an appreciation for other Christian communities. It should also help them understand the contributions that the Catholic Church can offer other Christians in the ecumenical movement. Ecumenical dialogue helps us appreciate the distinctiveness of Catholic teaching. Ecumenism, far from fostering religious indifferentism, gives a deeper understanding of the faith and an interest in knowing it in greater detail. More is discussed on this imperative in Chapter 6.

Dialogue is not an easy or simple enterprise, of course. In his book titled *Truth and Community*, Michael Kinnamon outlines elements that should characterize ecumenical dialogue:

1) Dialogue must have a spiritual orientation. A willingness to be transformed is essential.

2) Participants must be given permission to define themselves, to describe and witness to their faith in their own terms.

3) Participants need to have a clear understanding of their own faith and to present it with honesty and sincerity.

4) Participants need to treasure the integrity of

each person. As individuals speak, they must be mindful not only of their own integrity, but of the integrity of the persons with whom they may be disagreeing. Mutual growth, not victory, is the desired fruit.

5) Participants need to remember that dialogue is between people and not just between churches as institutions.

6) Participants need to understand past differences in terms of the present reality of our Christian partner. While we have to bear the responsibility, for example, of the evils of the Inquisition, the Crusades, or slavery, we must seek solutions for today in Christian truth.

7) Participants must be willing to separate essentials from nonessentials.

8) Participants should not insist on more agreement from partners in dialogue than they would expect from members of their own church.

9) Participants interpret the faith of the dialogue partner in its best, rather than in its worst, light.

10) As time goes on, dialogue does not avoid hard issues. Unfortunately, conversations will undoubtedly not want to tackle these difficult issues at first. Once trust has been established, however, it is important, in the service of truth, to discuss even difficult issues. In catechetical work, it will some-

times be necessary to clarify why we have
differed in the past to point out how we are
moving to overcome these differences.

11) Those in conversation should search for
ways to turn the increased understanding
achieved through dialogue into activities for
renewal. An immediate way to do this is to
have it lead to prayer. But as time goes on,
other activities may be possible.

Experiences of dialogue will vary according to age level
and capacity of the students. However, DREs can take the
lead in providing experiences of dialogue for themselves,
their catechists, and adults in their parishes. They can also
help their catechists stage dialogues that younger students
can follow to get the experience and to understand how it
is done. As Pope John Paul II reminds us, dialogue is a
spiritual discipline; ecumenical dialogue is a dialogue of
salvation, a means of deepening commitment to Christ
and to the Church (see *UUS*, #18, #82).

We have established that prayer and worship are central
to the ecumenical movement, as is the opportunity for
constructive dialogue. We now look at how the ecumenical movement provides doctrinal content for our catechesis. It helps in our understanding of Catholicism and its
teaching about itself, its history, and its goal of full communion. Catechesis draws on the ecumenical movement to
learn about our Catholic agreements with other churches.

As the Holy Father affirms, we share more with fellow
Christians than divides us (see *UUS*, #13, #14, #18). A
clear understanding of our Catholic teaching includes
knowing where we agree and where we still have issues to
resolve with other churches. This means that the results of
the dialogues are an important element in almost every
dimension of the catechetical enterprise. Chapters 4 and 5

speak more specifically to this part of catechetical ministry.

The *GDC* reminds us that "religious instruction in schools appear as a scholastic discipline with the same systematic demands and same rigor as other disciplines" (#73). Our parish education programs cannot be as rigorous and demanding as catechesis within the classroom of Catholic schools. Yet students can be helped to understand the importance and interest in the Catholic faith, including the results of ecumenical dialogue. DREs can introduce catechists to the results of these dialogues and their relevance to faith formation.

Motivated students can be helped to enhance their reading, experience, and knowledge of the other churches by being taught where to find the results of the dialogues. They also can be given an ecumenical perspective on developments in Catholic teaching and history. Students can "catch" enthusiasm for the knowledge of the faith from the catechist who finds Catholicism and its ecumenical program exciting. DREs can provide the kind of experiences that will help catechists "catch" the spirit as well as some of the content of ecumenical developments.

DIMENSIONS OF ALL FORMATION

The *Ecumenical Formation of Pastoral Workers* is explicit about the importance of infusing all catechetical work with the ecumenical vision of the Catholic Church. Three key dimensions of this pervasive vision are singled out:

1)   An *interpretive perspective* (hermeneutics) that "distinguishes between the *deposit of faith* and the ways these truths are formulated": It is important that Christians "understand each other and . . . explain their positions to each other," so that, where possible, formulations can be understood as "complementary rather than contradictory. . . In this way a common ecumenical language is emerging"

(*EFPW,* #9, #11; cf. *NCS,* #520.20; cf. *UUS,* #38).

For example, liturgical renewal and scholarship have made it possible for us to speak of an emerging common liturgical tradition in which the eucharistic prayers of Lutherans, Methodists, Catholics, Presbyterians, and Anglicans have begun to take on a common form and theological content. Significant eucharistic agreements have been reached with some of these churches.

Because Catholics believe that they are in real, if imperfect, communion with all baptized Christians, DREs should provide catechists and students with an interpretive horizon that sees unity where it exists, that is conducive to progressive steps taken together, and that carries a zeal for full visible unity. This specific issue is discussed further in Chapter 4.

2)   Faith taught within an understanding of the *hierarchy of truths*: The organizing and prioritizing of the truths within the whole development of the Christian faith "may also serve as a criterion for doctrinal formation in the church and be applied in such areas as spiritual life and popular devotion" (*EFPW,* #12).

An example of this is the clear priority Scripture has, for Catholics, in affirming tradition. Pope John Paul II notes: ". . . sacred Scripture, as the highest authority in matters of faith, and sacred tradition, is indispensable to the interpretation of the Word of God" (*UUS,* #79). Catholic understanding of Mary in the context of the unique mediatorship of Christ is another important example (see *NCS,* #520.07–09; *EFPW,* #12; *UUS,* #37; *GDC,* #114–115). These issues are treated in more detail in Chapter 5.

3)   Teaching that presents in a general way, according to the levels of those being trained, *the fruits of the dialogue,* noting the "distinctions used in agreed statements such a divergence and convergence, partial agreement, consensus,

and full agreement": These agreements need to "enter into the life of the church, renewing in certain ways that foster reconciliation" (*EFPW,* #13; *UUS,* #80).

The educational component of the process of ecumenical "reception" is essential (see *UUS,* #81). Practical ways of celebrating and understanding the results of the dialogues will require creativity on the part of the DRE, since we do not yet have detailed study guides for these theological results. The diocesan ecumenical officer is an important collaborator in this dimension of our catechist formation work. Other suggestions are made in Chapters 2, 4, and 5.

ELEMENTS FOR INCLUSION IN ECUMENICAL FORMATION

The *EFPW* details the more specific training in seminars, course work, and in-service programming that is recommended (#26). It includes more detail on themes that specialize in:

a)   biblical foundations: the theology of communion, God's plan for unity, the promise of the Holy Spirit, etc. (see *GDC,* #240–241);

b)   catholicity (universality) in time and place: the diversity of the Church in history, the variety of churches now in communion with Rome, episcopal collegiality, and the goal of full unity;

c)   doctrinal foundations (noted briefly in Chapter 1; *GDC,* #107);

d)   the history of ecumenism: early church divisions and attempts at resolution, the world and national councils, Catholic involvement, bilateral and multilateral dialogues, and key leaders (see *NCS,* #520.04, .05; *GDC,* #108).

e) purpose and method of ecumenism (discussed in this chapter and Chapter 1);

f) spiritual ecumenism;

g) other churches (discussed in Chapter 2);

h) areas for further dialogue (discussed in Chapters 5 and 6);

i) specific issues: worship, sacramental sharing, interchurch marriages, ministry and the role of women, and the role of the laity (discussed in Chapter 4);

j) ecumenism and mission (discussed in Chapter 6);

k) contemporary challenges: scientific developments, inculturation, proselytism, sects and new religious movements, faith, politics, nationalism and ethnicity, and secularism (see *GDC,* #109–113, #239).

Formal course work and even workshops may not be possible for all DREs or all catechists. The Bibliography notes some resources that can provide the needed background. Conferences can be arranged around some of these themes where catechists are in particular need of formation. It is important for DREs to follow the programs planned by the diocesan ecumenical officer and the diocesan commission to participate or help catechists participate where possible.

An enthusiastic spirit and the knowledge of where to find the content resources are most important. The skills for ecumenical formation and the understanding of methods of dialogue can be developed if there is a deep spiritual conversion to Christ's will for the Church and a receptivity to where Christians are being led on the pilgrimage toward full communion.

SUMMARY

To be effective catechetical leaders, DREs will want to develop confidence in and commitment to the Catholic approach to ecumenism and ecumenical formation. This will mean that DREs' spiritual life and doctrinal formation are informed by zeal for the unity of the Church and knowledge of ecumenical developments.

Specifically, Catholic catechists will develop an interpretive perspective in everything that is taught that will serve the unity of the Church. DREs will help catechists help their students see how this dimension of Catholic identity touches every area of Catholic life.

In doctrinal instruction, the hierarchy of truths will be an essential element in the way the truths of the faith are transmitted and understood. The results of the dialogues with particular churches will inform instruction where appropriate.

DREs seriously pursuing their vocation will find that it is a process of life-long learning. The elements of ecumenical formation provide a rich challenge for deepening the faith, and opportunities for dialogue provide occasions for spiritual enrichment.

FOR REFLECTION

1. What have been your experiences of prayer or spiritual sharing with other Christians? Where have you experienced dialogue between Christians? Where in your life can you deepen your experience of prayer and dialogue

with other Christians?

2. Of all the elements enumerated as importation for ecumenical formation, which are the easiest to integrate into Catholic catechesis? Which are the most challenging?

3. What suggestions would you offer for improving the ecumenical dimension of the catechist formation programs with which you work?

4 Sacramental Catechesis in Ecumenical Perspective

One of my colleagues is an active member of Holy Trinity parish, Georgetown. He came into the office one day, saying that he was practically run down in the aisle at church. It seems he inadvertently barred the way of some of the candidates who, having been called to the altar to receive the Word of God (Bibles) in one of the rites of initiation, were being dismissed from the Eucharist with the catechumens. Apparently, baptized candidates for full communion were included with catechumens in the rites, which are designed for the uncatechized and the unbaptized.

Years ago, many parishes mixed candidates for full communion with bona fide unbaptized catechumens. It created confusion for the congregation and was a violation of the directives of the Rite of Christian Initiation of Adults (RCIA) itself. Fortunately, as our catechetical approaches to the RCIA have matured, this mistake has been occurring less and less frequently.

We have experienced a successful catechetical renewal in the RCIA development in recent years. Coming to us are Catholics who are baptized and uncatechized, Christians who are baptized and uncatechized, Christians who are firm believers but seek full communion with the Catholic Church, and even Christians who want to "transfer" to the Catholic Church but do not see the need for initiation.

All of this requires specific training for the RCIA team, and special preparation for the variety of catechumens and candidates. DREs carry an important role in this sacramental formation.

This chapter will touch on 1) the "history and essential principles of the Church's liturgical and sacramental life" (*NCS*, #532.301); 2) "the Eucharist as the source and summit of the Christian life" (*NCS*, #532.303); 3) "the meaning, structure, and implementation of principles of the *Rite of Christian Initiation* of Adults" (*NCS*, #532.306); 4) issues related to Matrimony; 5) teaching about ordination; and 6) other issues of ecumenical importance in sacramental catechesis.

We will look at the theological basis for sharing in worship, the place of Baptism and the RCIA in ecumenical formation, sacramental sharing and eucharistic agreement, concerns about preparation for Matrimony, and some other suggestions.

THE CENTRALITY OF WORSHIP IN OUR LIFE TOGETHER AS CHURCHES

The liturgical renewal has brought back the balance in Catholic life between Word and Sacrament, between private devotion and public worship, between participation by the congregation and leadership of the celebrant. This biblical and liturgical renewal is a shared return to the sources of all the Western churches in the ecumenical movement (see *NCS*, #532.301–302). In preparing catechists to teach liturgy and sacraments, DREs will want to be sure that catechists know this common renewal and its importance for our life together as churches, so that they can communicate it to their students.

Catholic worship has become more participatory, more biblical, and more eucharistic. This is not because Catholics are copying the Orthodox or the Reformation churches, although the Church has learned a great deal from them. Rather, by moving closer to Christ, to the Fathers and the Great Tradition, and to the core of our sacramental and biblical faith, we have come closer to our fellow Christians who are renewing their own churches and its worship.

Quoting the Second Vatican Council, the Holy Father acknowledges that the churches separated from the Catholic Church are truly means of salvation, truly sacramental, even though we are not yet able to realize full sacramental communion with them:

> With reference to the many positive elements present in the other churches and Ecclesial Communities, the Decree [on Ecumenism] adds: 'All of these, which come from Christ and lead back to him, belong by right to the one Church of Christ. The separated brethren also carry out many of the sacred actions of the Christian religion. Undoubtedly, in many ways that vary according to the condition of each Church or Community, these actions can truly engender a life of grace, and can be rightly described as capable of providing access to the community of salvation'. (*UUS*, #13)

In today's religious situation it is important that educators in all of our Christian churches work to help the sacramental life and the communal character of the Christian faith come alive. Catechists are competing with a materialistic and ethically relativist culture for the attention of the young generation—a generation that is open to spiritual values if these are understood individually and subjectively (see *GDC*, #25). However, Catholic catechesis and the ecumenical movement have the challenge of renewing the community and sacramental sense of the Christian faith among our people.

In the following sections we will review both sacramental understanding and sacramental practice as they are taught by the catechist in light of Catholic ecumenical principles and our progress together toward full communion.

BAPTISM

Differences over Baptism—between Anabaptists and Baptists who only baptize confessing adults and more sacramental Protestant, Orthodox, Anglican, and Catholic churches who baptize infants—is one of the major issues dividing the churches. Catholic return to a focus on Baptism of adults and the importance of a living faith in the family of the infant to be baptized contribute to building on a common understanding of Baptism.

The WCC *Baptism, Eucharist and Ministry* statement enables Christians to say together:

> While the possibility that infant baptism was also practiced in the apostolic age cannot be excluded, baptism upon profession of faith is the most clearly attested pattern in the New Testament documents. . . . Both the baptism of believers and the baptism of infants take place in the Church as the community of faith. . . . All baptism is rooted in and declares Christ's faithfulness unto death. It has its setting within the life and faith of the Church and, through the witness of the whole Church, points to the faithfulness of God, ground of all life in faith. (#11–12)

The full text of *BEM* is brief and readable and should

provide a useful resource in working with adults and catechists. It is a convergence text and does not claim to reach
full consensus. It is particularly helpful with couples
preparing for an interchurch wedding, especially if there
are no particular documents between the Catholic Church
and the church of the spouse.

Baptism provides the common ground for all ecumenical work, as is noted in the *Directory for the Application of
Principles and Norms on Ecumenism* (*DAPN*, see #92–101;
also *UUS*, #6, #12, #42). Although every Baptism, in what-
ever church, is Baptism into Christ and into his Church,
we do not yet celebrate an "ecumenical Baptism," properly
so called.

The Baptism of a child of an interchurch family should
be celebrated in the integrity of the worship of one church
into which the child is registered. Those involved in baptismal preparation should be knowledgeable about the
parameters of ecumenical participation in a baptism, in a
Catholic ceremony or in another church.

Where a Baptism is performed in the congregation of
one member of an interchurch couple, provisions may be
made for introducing the child with celebration as a new
Christian in the parish of the spouse. Careful planning,
however, needs to take into account the involvement of
parents in congregations of separate churches. Matrimonial preparation for interchurch couples will also need to
reflect on the baptismal practices of the two churches to
which they belong.

Every Christian will be impelled by the faith to do
everything in their power to raise their children Christian
in the church that their conscience shows them to be true.
Catholics make a verbal promise to this effect, which they
share with their prospective spouse (see *DAPN*, #150–151).
It is recognized, of course, that the spouse may have a
similar conviction, so no penalties are imposed on the

Catholic party should the child be raised in the spouse's church. The stability of the family and the Christian upbringing of the child remain primary values for the Church.

The Rite of Christian Initiation for Adults (RCIA) has been an important element of Catholic renewal. It helps Catholics meet some of the criticisms of reformers in the past and build bridges among Christians today (see *GDC*, #90, #256–258).

Even though the Catholic approach to other churches is to engage in dialogue toward full communion, individuals will decide to join the Catholic Church before such communion is achieved (see *DAPN*, #99). Thus, pastoral leaders must make a clear distinction between the baptized candidates for full communion, baptized but uncatechized Catholics, and catechumens *per se* in planning, ritualization, and formation.

However, in many parishes, up to half of those involved in the process of initiation are not catechumens. Catholics are challenged to take our baptismal theology seriously. RCIA leaders need to provide the necessary ecumenical sensitivity and bring all those in initiation processes in the community into deeper contact with the mainstream of congregational and Catholic life (see Ronald A. Oakham, *One at the Table: The Reception of Baptized Christians*, Liturgy Training Publications).

The Rite itself provides a special service for the reception into full communion of those who are already baptized:

> This is the liturgical rite by which a person born and baptized in a separated ecclesial community is received, according to the Latin rite, into the full communion of the Catholic Church. The rite is so arranged that *no greater burden than necessary . . . is required for the establishment of communion and unity.* (*RCIA*, #473; emphasis added)

Nevertheless, many Christians coming to the Catholic Church need as much serious initiation as the individual who has no Christian background whatsoever. They need to know the distinctive claims of the Catholic faith and understand its ecumenical mission and openness. For example, we have some Anglican and Protestant Christians with a denominational understanding of church who see no need for special initiation. They simply want to *transfer* into the Catholic Church, as one might move from a parish in one city to a parish in another city when relocating. These people will need to understand the sacramental, hierarchical, and ecumenical character of Catholicism.

On the other hand, there are those who come from more sectarian, even fundamentalist, backgrounds who have a view of the Catholic Church that may be more rigid and literalistic than is the tradition. Catechists will have to help these people see Catholicism's openness to biblical scholarship, its theological and cultural inclusiveness, and its ecumenical commitments.

Christians coming into full communion must be distinguished in programs, rites, and spiritual approaches from those who are not Christian. Many of them will need serious catechesis. DREs can help in this discernment process, depending on their particular role in the RCIA team.

Christians presenting themselves for full communion with the Catholic Church will build on the faith nurtured in other communities. Acknowledging the gifts the Catholic Church receives from the church of the new Catholic may ritualize this. Opportunities should be provided for the new Catholic to study the relationship of the Catholic Church to his or her previous church, and the hopes or challenges we have in moving toward full communion.

Finally, all participants in the RCIA, catechumens or candidates, will need to be given the opportunity to understand the Catholic Church's ecumenical commitments.

This will include its relationships to churches in the local community (see *NCS*, #532.306).

THE EUCHARIST

The Eucharist, the normal Sunday service for Anglicans, Orthodox, and Catholics, is central to the life of the Christian (see *NCS*, #532.301, #532.303). Many of the Reformers revised the Eucharistic Liturgy so that there would be less frequent communion, celebrating it only when the congregation was able to receive. As a result, it has only been with the modern ecumenical movement that weekly Eucharist has become more central in Protestant life. Similarly, Catholics have begun to receive the Eucharist more frequently; on occasion, both the Body and Blood of Christ are received, as the Reformers desired. In fact, all the ecumenically attentive Western churches have begun to renew their Eucharistic Liturgy to become more faithful to the tradition, and thus to come closer to one another.

The key differences at the time of the Reformation concerned the real presence of Christ in the Eucharist, or the manner of the real presence. There were also controversies concerning the understanding of the relationship of the one sacrifice of Christ on the cross and the relationship of that sacrifice to its celebration in the Mass.

With Lutherans and Anglicans, Catholics have reached agreement on both of these issues (see *GA*). Disagreements on Holy Orders, however, make it impossible to celebrate together or to receive at one another's altars. With Reformed, Methodist, and Disciples churches we have developed a high level of convergence, if not full agreement (see *GA* and *DC*).

In the multilateral dialogue of many churches in conversation through the World Council, the *BEM* text produces a remarkable ten-page convergence statement, which has found wide reception among the churches. It is important for DREs and catechists to read this statement, preferably in an ecumenical context. This will help them know how it is understood in other churches.

Among other things, this text states:

> The Eucharist is essentially the sacrament of the gift which God makes to us in Christ through the power of the Holy Spirit. Every Christian receives this gift of salvation through communion in the body and blood of Christ. . . . The Eucharist is the sacrament of the unique sacrifice of Christ, who ever lives to make intercession for us. . . . Christ's mode of presence in the Eucharist is unique. . . . While Christ's real presence in the Eucharist does not depend on the faith of the individual, all agree that to discern the body and blood of Christ, faith is required. . . . The Spirit makes the crucified and risen Christ really present. . . . It is in virtue of the living word of Christ and by the power of the Holy Spirit that the bread and wine become the sacramental signs of Christ's body and blood. . . . The Eucharist involves the believer in the central event of the world's history. (#2, #4, #8, #14)

This text and the others concluded between Catholics, Orthodox, Lutherans, Anglicans, Methodists, and Reformed are a rich source of spiritual blessing for all our churches. They form a basis for renewing our people's faith in the real presence of Christ and in our participation in the one sacrifice of Christ on the cross. It is important to recognize that ecumenical renewal should deepen our appreciation of the sacramental life of the churches and impel us to hunger for the day when we can celebrate the Eucharist together.

Over two hundred churches have responded to *BEM*. The theologically trained educators will find the five volumes of responses, including that of the Catholic Church, to be important contributions to our understanding of one another and to clarifying what further work will be necessary before full eucharistic communion is restored.

In fostering a deeper understanding of Christ's presence in the Eucharist, catechists help their students feel the urgency for full eucharistic communion among all Christians every time we receive at our separate tables in our divisions. Every time we approach the altar we pray for the day when full eucharistic communion can be celebrated among the churches.

Sacramental sharing, especially the Eucharist, is a sign of the unity the Church has achieved. For the Orthodox, this principle holds priority. Yet eucharistic communion in Christ also builds up the unity among the churches. For the Eastern and most Oriental Orthodox, however, sharing the Eucharist in this way is not possible.

For Catholics, on the other hand, the level of faith and sacramental life we share with these sister churches would permit an easier sharing of Eucharist, Reconciliation, and Anointing of the Sick (see *DAPN*, #122–128). It is important to respect the faith and practice of Orthodox believers in our schools and communities.

An exception is the Syrian Church of Antioch (Oriental Orthodox). We have reciprocal eucharistic hospitality as a result of the common declaration of Pope John Paul II and Patriarch Ignatius in 1981. This sharing is encouraged at marriages between Syrians and Catholics in India. When the other Orthodox Christians request Communion and are properly disposed, Catholics cannot refuse them. We should help them consult with their priests and learn the doctrine and practice of their own church.

The Holy Father says about sacramental sharing:

> In this context, it is a source of joy to note that Catholic ministers are able, in certain particular cases, to administer the Sacraments of the Eucharist, Penance and Anointing of the Sick to Christians who are not in full communion with the Catholic Church but who greatly desire to receive these sacraments, freely request them and manifest the faith which the Catholic Church professes with regard to these sacraments. Conversely, in specific cases and in particular circumstances, Catholics too can request these same sacraments from ministers of Churches in which these sacraments are valid. The conditions for such reciprocal reception have been laid down in specific norms [in *DAPN*]; for the sake of furthering ecumenism these norms must be respected. (*UUS*, #46; reference added)

The situation with the Reformation churches is even more complex because of the diversity of theologies of the sacraments and the lack of reciprocity. Even when, in exceptional situations, Protestants can receive the Eucharist from a Catholic minister, Catholics do not receive the Eucharist in Protestant churches because we do not yet recognize the ordinations in any of the Reformation churches.

When they are being instructed about the sacraments, it is important for Catholics to learn how Catholic doctrine differs from the doctrine of other churches, where we share belief, what Catholic sacramental practices are and why we observe them, and what the sacramental practices are of other churches. This instruction, of course, will be adapted to the age level and capacity of each class being catechized. However, it is important to note that our practice follows our understanding of the sacraments and is not merely a matter of rules.

Unlike the Orthodox, we do not exclude all cases of sacramental sharing. Unlike many of our Protestant partners, on the other hand, we do not promote open communion. It is not correct to say that eucharistic sharing is never possible for either Orthodox or Protestants—nor is it correct to issue a general invitation.

The levels of agreements in the dialogues, especially in the case of Lutherans and Anglicans, need to be taken into account in catechesis and application of the Norms of the Church. Toward this end, it will be helpful for DREs to work with catechists of other churches so that the Catholic position can be made clear in their classes and their churches' positions can be clear for our students. Christian educators from all of the ecumenically oriented churches can work together to enhance the sacramental faith in all our people, especially concerning Christ's presence in the Eucharist.

The conditions for administering the sacraments of Eucharist, Penance, and Anointing of the Sick are quite clear and should be made known to both Catholics and fellow Christians. Prospective recipients must:

1) ask for the sacrament on their own initiative;

2) manifest the Catholic faith in the sacrament;

3) be properly disposed;

4) display a spiritual need for the sacrament.
   (*DAPN*, #130–131)

Obviously, the middle of Mass is not the time to enter into this process of discernment if a fellow Christian asks whether or not communion is possible. In such a case the individual should be invited to enter into conversation with a properly instructed catechist or other Catholic minister to determine whether the occasion is appropriate and all of the guidelines apply.

The *DAPN* and the Code of Canon Law specify that "a Catholic minister may administer" these three sacraments of Eucharist, Penance, and Anointing of the Sick, but it also specifies that bishops and episcopal conferences may establish further guidelines, including reserving the pastoral discernment to diocesan leadership under the bishop. Although there are no U.S. episcopal conference guidelines, a brief note appears in the missalette. Our catechists and students need to know that guidelines may vary in different dioceses and in different parts of the world.

Since this is a pastoral decision, made in common between the prospective communicant and the Catholic minister, it is important that pastoral leadership be carefully prepared for this task. This involves knowing the results of past and ongoing dialogues, the spiritualities of our ecumenical partners, and the practices of partner churches. For example, it can be presumed that Anglicans and Lutherans, if they are in harmony with the faith of their church, believe in Christ's real presence, however, individual cases may differ. On the other hand, although there are Methodists and Presbyterians whose faith is in harmony with the Catholic faith, there are those who reject Catholic understandings of Christ's presence. These individuals would not be disposed to receive the Eucharist as we understand it.

Generally speaking, Catholics need to exercise special sensitivity in celebrating Eucharist, Penance, and Anointing of the Sick in other churches. In Orthodox churches, for example, Catholics can celebrate these sacraments but should refrain, out of respect for the understanding of the Church and the sacraments in the Orthodox churches. On the other hand, some Protestant churches invite all baptized and properly disposed Christians to the Eucharist. This practice is based on a theology of the Lord's Supper that affirms the table as Christ's and that particular churches do not have the authority to exclude baptized Christians. This practice is called *open communion*.

While Catholics do not share this understanding of the Church and the Eucharist, we recognize that this is a practice, at least among Methodists, that goes back over two hundred years and is not meant to be offensive to those of us with different understandings of the relationship of eucharistic communion to full ecclesial communion. Catholics are respectful of the Eucharist in other churches and may approach the altar to receive a blessing from the presiding minister, but we have not yet come to recognize the ordination in any of the Reformation churches and therefore cannot yet acknowledge the fullness of sacramental reality in their eucharistic celebrations.

In many communities where ecumenical relationships are well developed and Christians understand one another's eucharistic practice, the individual who is unable to communicate at a Eucharist of another church will go up and receive a blessing. When the Holy Father visited Sweden, he was moved when the Archbishop of Uppsala came forward for such a blessing. In England, the Cardinal of Westminster will receive a blessing from the Archbishop of Canterbury during an Anglican liturgy, and the archbishop will come forward for a blessing from the cardinal during Catholic Communion.

MATRIMONY

Preparing young people to understand the sacrament of Matrimony and assisting couples in proximate preparation for their own wedding is an important dimension of sacramental catechesis, especially since Catholic understanding differs so markedly from the secular culture and some of the Protestant churches. In some communities, matrimonial preparation becomes an occasion for evangelization for the uncatechized or inactive Catholic. Sensitivity is especially important in preparing those entering into an interchurch union.

Matrimonial preparation programs will be served well by including on the team several couples who are successful interchurch families, where both of the spouses are active in their different Christian churches and the children have been raised amicably as good Christians. Child-rearing is one of the most challenging dimensions of interchurch family life, but one least likely to be apparent to those deeply in love and preparing for Matrimony. Couples with positive experiences in working through their differences and coming to a common mind on nurturing the Christian faith of their children are important resources in matrimonial preparation. These couples are able to witness out of their own experience and struggles and can explain how some challenging situations are dealt with in ways that enhance their faith and deepen their commitment to each other and to Christ.

The 1993 ecumenical *DAPN* singles out the interchurch wedding as a specific example of sacramental sharing (#143–160). Whether there is a dispensation from form and the wedding takes place in a Protestant, Orthodox, or Anglican service—or it is a Catholic service, with priest or deacon as principal witness—care needs to be taken to be as ecumenically inclusive as possible.

A Mass is discouraged at an interchurch wedding, though it is not impossible (see *DAPN*, #159). However, if a Mass is celebrated, sensitivity needs to be taken about the diversity of the congregation. The question of eucharistic sharing needs to be handled responsibly and with care.

The Church needs to find ways to nurture the faith of couples in interchurch families. Often, when both spouses are active in their churches, they can become strong ecumenical leaders. Likewise, the results of the dialogues are important resources for preparing couples for an interchurch wedding—if they are religiously interested—and in nurturing the interchurch family. The zeal for the unity of the Church has a particular urgency in families with active members in different Christian churches. Educational programming in the parish must be attentive to the needs of these couples and the resource they provide for ecumenical interest and spiritual nurture of other interchurch couples who may experience strains on their relationship.

It is also important to realize that Orthodox, Anglican, and Protestant churches have different approaches to remarriage after the dissolution of an earlier marriage. While this has not been considered a divisive issue for the Church (see *OO*, *Ox*, and *ARC 2*), it causes a great deal of strain and anguish in some relationships. Because the annulment process is difficult for other Christians to understand, careful catechesis and sensitivity are important when this sad necessity arises.

Some dioceses have interchurch marriage guidelines for their people, sometimes with particular churches. It is important for DREs and catechists to know these and, where appropriate, use them in instruction about Matrimony. While there are no national U.S. guidelines with any churches, except the Syrian and Armenians (see *OO*), there are suggestions for Orthodox-Catholic weddings (see USCC, *A Guide on Catholic-Orthodox Marriages for Catholic Clergy and Other Pastoral Ministers; Ox*, and *BU*). The Canadian bishops, Anglican and Catholic, have produced some suggestions that can be useful in the U.S. (see *ARC 2*).

ORDINATION

Other than Baptism, Catholics do not receive the sacraments in emergencies from Protestant ministers and Anglican priests because we do not yet fully recognize the sacrament of Holy Orders in these churches. Major progress has been made, however, in the dialogues toward a common doctrine of Holy Orders. Anglicans and Lutherans do not usually speak of ordination as a sacrament, but the dialogues have shown that we are not in disagreement about the biblical doctrine and necessity of ordination (see *GA*).

Our most developed agreement on the three-fold ministry of bishops, priests, and deacons is with the Anglican Church. In 1988, Cardinal Willebrands said that a "new context" existed for the evaluation of Anglican Orders, and in 1994 Cardinal Cassidy said that no further work was necessary on our common understanding of Eucharist and ordained ministry. Obviously, our differences over the ordination of women make it impossible to act on these agreements at the present time, though the Holy Father continues to encourage ecumenical dialogue on this subject (see *ARC 2*).

While Catholics do not yet have full communion in the sacramental ministry of the ordained, we do not deny the ministerial importance and efficacy of Protestant and Anglican clergy. Rather, we speak of a "lack" or "incompleteness" from our point of view, a lack that Catholics and Protestants are called to work together to overcome. The *Ministry* section of *BEM* has been an important contribution to the discussion of all their churches about their hopes for agreement on ordination, but it has been much less successful than either *Baptism* or *Eucharist*.

It is important for Catholics to know ministers and priests of other Christian communities, to respect them, and to look forward to the day when we can celebrate one united ministry around the eucharistic table.

OTHER SACRAMENTS

The Orthodox have not traditionally numbered and ordered the sacraments in the same way that the West has. It was only in the Middle Ages when Catholic theologians settled on the number seven. However, Catholics recognize Orthodox sacraments, the common centrality of the Eucharist, and the importance of the hierarchical ordering of the local church around the bishop at the center of the eucharistic community (see *Ox*).

The Reformation churches spoke of only two sacraments, Baptism and Eucharist, though Lutherans also retained a third, Reconciliation. The reason for this was that sacraments were defined as those rites explicitly instituted by the historical Jesus as attested to in Scripture. Catholics, of course, also affirm the centrality of these two sacraments and relate the other five to them.

In teaching about sacraments in a Protestant seminary, I always found that my students were interested in studying all seven sacraments, since all their ministries entail ordination, Reconciliation, Confirmation, Matrimony, and ministry to the sick, some even with anointing. When the rites in their renewed form, the history, and the Catholic definition are explained, many Protestants find that their sacramental understanding is not foreign to what they believe and practice. Some interchurch couples in Marriage Encounter are comfortable explaining, together, the sacramentality of their union.

I even had some African American Baptist students who found *transubstantiation* a helpful way of explaining what they believed about how Christ is present in the Lord's Supper. Their understanding flowed from their deep piety, a literalistic interpretation of the biblical narrative, and a clear and contemporary explanation of what Catholics mean by *substance* and *accidents* as technical terms in a scholastic system, rather than the common-sense meanings we may give to these terms in our modern scientific parlance.

Christians share a great deal in their sacramental understanding of God's working in our lives through the Church and its worship. Through dialogue and experience of one another's worship, we are beginning to be transformed in our mutual understanding—and by coming closer to Christ, we come closer to one another. Catholic students need to see the joy and struggle of this process as an important component of their sacramental catechesis.

SUMMARY

Christians share a great deal in the sacramental understanding of the nature of the Church and its worship. The significant differences need to be clear in catechesis, in the context of what is shared, and in our mutual hope for full sacramental reconciliation. Catholic doctrine and practice are communicated through catechesis in such a way as to nurture a deep ecumenical spirituality.

Baptism is the common ground of ecumenical commitment. Baptismal preparation and the RCIA need to be ecumenically sensitive to the status of all candidates and their Christian formation and must provide appropriate ecumenical formation for those who would take on Catholic ecumenical responsibility.

Eucharistic catechesis creates a profound faith in Christ's presence, a deep eucharistic hunger for full communion, and an appropriate understanding—according to age level and capacity—of Catholic ecumenical sacramental teaching and that of ecumenical partners.

Matrimonial catechesis and wedding preparation for interchurch couples need to be informed by the experience of successful interchurch families, the levels of agreement reached among the churches to which the couples belong, and the ecumenical understanding and practices of the churches.

Instruction about ordained ministry and the other sacraments needs to take account of our understanding of one another and our hopes for full reconciliation. Christians can learn from one another's sacramental practices and work together as educators to deepen the sacramental faith of our people and their hopes for full reconciliation.

While DREs may not be involved in all the parish sacramental programs, they carry a particularly important leadership role in knowing where the Catholic Church is on these matters and how the various sacramental catechetical programs serve the common vision of the parish and total Catholic Church. It may seem like a challenge, but it is also a spiritually vital learning opportunity.

FOR REFLECTION

1. How has the liturgical renewal enriched the life of your parish? How has it enriched the other Christian communities in your neighborhood? How can we collaborate in renewing the worship of all the churches together?

2. What issues of sacramental formation in your parish are shared with other churches? What can be done together to deepen sacramental understanding among Christians?

3. How ecumenically sensitive are the rites of initiation in your parish? What can your parish do to support couples preparing for or living in interchurch families?

5 Implementations of the Dialogues for Catechesis

When I was teaching Church and Sacrament to a class at Memphis Theological Seminary in 1974, with several DREs who were candidates for the Master of Religious Education in Roman Catholic Studies, we were challenged to find materials that gave an ecumenical view of the sacraments and the Church. We had a great time looking at one another's liturgical books, exploring the different ways we told the story of the Reformation, and sharing our respective understandings of the Church and its unity. It was especially satisfying to see how the Protestants were able to profit by an ecumenically sensitive Catholic explanation of the "other five" sacraments.

By 1975, the World Council of Churches had published, with full Catholic participation, its vision of a united Church as a *Conciliar Fellowship* (*Communion*) further elaborated by 1991 in the text *The Church as Koinonia: Gift and Calling* (*WCC93*). During the 1970s, both Anglicans and Lutherans developed agreements with Catholics on Baptism and Eucharist, and made progress on agreements regarding ordination. By the 1990s, all the major Western churches, Catholic and Protestant, had renewed their liturgical texts so that parallel eucharistic prayers can be found in most of our worship books, grounded in a common theology. In the 1980s, convergence positions emerged among Catholics, Methodists, and Reformed, and the WCC published its historic *Baptism, Eucharist and Ministry (BEM)* statement, to which over two hundred churches—Orthodox, Protestant, Anglican, and Catholic—responded.

There are now dialogues with Pentecostals, Baptists, and Evangelicals that touch on some of these issues. For every doctrinal course a DRE might take—like the one I taught on Church and Sacraments—there are ample resources in the bilateral dialogues (theological agreements between two churches) and the multilateral dialogues (dialogues between several churches, for example, within the WCC) to inform our understanding of the Catholic tradition and our teaching of the ecumenical progress to date.

Today, Church and Sacraments can be easily taught in an ecumenical context, recognizing commonalities of doctrine and practice, respecting differences, and noting progress toward full reconciliation. In this chapter we will note agreements that touch on how one can teach such themes as 1) revelation; 2) the nature of the Church and its unity; 3) the hierarchical nature of the Church; 4) Christ; and 5) Our Lady (see *NCS*, #520.01–.11, #520.20–.21).

The Holy Father is particularly concerned that catechists take their role in incorporating the results of ecumenical progress into Catholic instruction. "At the stage which we have now reached, this process of *mutual enrichment* must be taken seriously into account" (*UUS*, #87; emphasis added); ". . . a new task lies before us: that of *receiving the results* already achieved" which "must involve the whole people of God." Results are not to remain "statements of bilateral commissions but must become a *common heritage*" (*UUS*, #80; emphasis added). Before students can fully assimilate these results, DREs will want to know what has been done and help adapt it to the age levels of students and the particular contexts of the parishes (see *GDC,* #30, #34 ff.).

SCRIPTURE AND TRADITION

The Second Vatican Council document entitled the *Dogmatic Constitution on Divine Revelation* (*Dei verbum*) renewed Catholic focus on the role of Scripture and the appropriate relationship of tradition and the magisterium to it. The Holy Father outlines this renewed focus in laying out his ecumenical agenda, when he proposes for dialogue: "the relationship between Sacred Scripture, as the highest authority in matters of faith, and Sacred Tradition, as indispensable to the interpretation of the Word of God" (*UUS,* #79).

The biblical renewal has been one of the richest contributions of contemporary catechesis (see *NCS,* #520.01, #520.10–.12; #532.101–.102). Virtually all biblical scholars working from an ecclesiastically sensitive perspective are using the same sources and coming to the same conclusions for the churches. This revitalization of Scripture scholarship and catechesis is one gift we have received from the Reformation churches. Our common methods and perspectives have enabled us to overcome important differences of the past (see *CCC,* #78, #81, #82, #113, #119; *GDC,* #36–45).

Catholic students will want to learn to share Bible study with their fellow Christians of other traditions and to recognize the love for the Scriptures in the Protestant churches. It will also be important for students to distinguish between a literalistic interpretation on the one hand, popular among some churches called "fundamentalist" (see *GDC,* #201), and a reductive approached used by some scholars, like some in the Jesus Seminar (see *GDC,* #95–97).

While the Fathers at the Second Vatican Council were teaching on the Catholic understanding of Scripture and tradition in the context of the doctrine of revelation, the WCC, with full Catholic participation, was finding a common ground on this issue that was so divisive at the time of the Reformation. A deeper sense of tradition in the formation of Scripture enabled the scholars to see the role of the Holy Spirit in a new way:

> The oral and written tradition of the prophets and apostles under the guidance of the Holy Spirit led to the formation of Scriptures and to the canonization of the Old and New Testaments as the Bible of the Church. The very fact that Tradition precedes the Scriptures points to the significance of tradition, but also to the Bible as the treasure of the Word of God. (*FO*, #42)

This World Conference, held in Montreal in 1963, convened during the Council. It is useful to study its statement *Scripture, Tradition and the Traditions* side by side with the Council's *Dogmatic Constitution on Divine Revelation*, to note the dramatic convergence that emerged.

The affirmation of the "traditional" character of Scripture at Montreal is further amplified by its explication of the "traditioning" process in the Church:

> Our starting point is that we are all living in a tradition which goes back to our Lord and has its roots in the Old Testament, and we are all indebted to that tradition inasmuch as we have received the revealed truth, the Gospel, through its being transmitted from one generation to another. Thus we can say that we exist as Christians by the Tradition of the Gospel (the *paradosis* of the *kerygma*) testified in Scripture, transmitted in and by the Church through the power of the Holy Spirit. Tradition taken in this sense is actualized in the preaching of the Word,

in administration of the Sacraments and worship, in Christian teaching and theology, and in
mission and witness to Christ by the lives of the
members of the Church. (*FO*, #45)

This dramatic breakthrough does not, of course, solve
all the church-dividing problems of biblical interpretation,
the theology and administration of teaching authority in
the Church. Neither does it settle the process of discernment between the traditions (with a small t) and the Tradition of the Gospel (with a large T). The latter is seen to be
normative for all within a united Church, the former are
expressions of the appropriate diversity of the churches.

THE NATURE OF THE CHURCH AND ITS UNITY

Since the Second Vatican Council, the renewed Catholic
view of the Church as a communion has gradually been
assimilated into catechesis, with emphases on the centrality of the People of God; its sacramental character; collegiality among its bishops; co-responsibility of bishops,
priests, and laity; and the contribution the Catholic
Church makes to the unity we seek (see *CCC*, #815, #816,
#820–22, #838, #846–48, #870, #875, #877, #1445). The
"ecclesial nature of catechesis" will impel DREs to help
catechists understand all that is taught against the horizon
of the Church and its way on the pilgrimage toward unity
(see *GDC*, #105–106).

In his encyclical, Pope John Paul II outlines those elements under discussion as we seek full communion:

. . . areas in need of fuller study before a true
consensus of faith can be achieved: 1) the relationship between sacred Scripture, as the highest authority in matters of faith, and sacred
tradition, as indispensable to the interpretation

of the Word of God; 2) the Eucharist, as the
sacrament of the body and blood of Christ, and
offering of praise to the Father . . . ; 3) Ordination . . . ; 4) the magisterium of the Church . . .
;5) the Virgin Mary, as Mother of God and icon
of the Church. (*UUS*, #79)

The WCC, like many of the bilateral conversations
including most of the ones in which the Catholic Church
is involved, has outlined a vision of visible unity that
would entail similar elements of full communion:

The unity of the church to which we are called
is a *koinonia* given and expressed in 1) the common confession of the apostolic faith; 2) a common sacramental life entered by the one
baptism and celebrated together in one
eucharistic fellowship; 3) a common life in
which members and ministries are mutually recognized and reconciled; and 4) a common mission witnessing to the Gospel of God's grace to
all people and serving the whole of creation.
The goal of the search for full communion is
realized when all the churches are able to recognize in one another the one, holy, catholic and
apostolic church in its fullness. This full communion will be 5) expressed on the local level
and the universal levels through conciliar forms
of life and action. In such communion churches
are bound in all aspects of life together at all
levels in confessing the one faith and engaging
in worship and witness, deliberation and action.
(*WCC93*; numbers and emphasis added)

In teaching the nature of the Church, these elements
and the agreements that exist among the churches regarding them need to be taken into account. The diocesan

ecumenical officer and local Christian ministers and colleagues can help catechists in relating the particular dialogues and elements of teaching to each of the five areas enunciated by Pope John Paul II and by the churches together in the WCC.

DREs will have an important role in facilitating understanding of how far we have come in each area with particular churches and how these various dimensions of the Church and its unity relate to one another.

When working with more mature students, young people from other churches can be brought together with fellow educators to consider what hopes we have together, what it would mean to live in full communion, and what contributions the particular dialogues have made. Catechists can arrange students into a "mini" Vatican Council III, where Christians meet together to consider how far we have come on the road to unity and what concrete steps can be recommended for the future. Such an exercise would help students take concrete responsibility for thinking through the ecumenical future of the Church on this pilgrimage, and envision themselves as future leaders in the Church.

AUTHORITY AND LEADERSHIP IN THE CHURCH

In addition to the sacramental area, one of the most challenging dimensions of our differences concerns how decisions are made and what is involved in the respective roles of bishops, the pope, and laity. Orthodox, Anglicans, and Catholics claim bishops ordained in the apostolic succession, and the authority of the early councils of the Church.

Protestant churches, on the other hand, govern themselves through collegial and conciliar structures, most with various levels of communion: local, global, and national.

Catholics, of course, bring the role of the bishop of Rome into the discussion, both as a service of the unity of the Church and carrying a heritage of affirming infallibility and universal and ordinary jurisdiction. At the First Vatican Council (1869–1870), the infallibility and jurisdiction of the pope in the Church was defined as a dogma. When the Orthodox and Catholic churches lived together for a thousand years, and at the time of the sixteenth-century Reformation, this was not a binding teaching of the Church, though Catholics claim it is rooted in the heritage of the Church from biblical times.

DREs need sufficient study of the history of Church governance if they are to communicate to students and catechists that the way the Catholic Church is governed now is not the way it has always been governed. There were one thousand years of full communion between East and West, where the papal claims were never accepted in the East. Many Roman Catholic claims were only clarified after the divisions of East and West and the Reformation.

The vision of unity proposed by theologians representing their churches, including the Catholic Church, in the WCC's Faith and Order Commission for a united Church, is a *Conciliar Fellowship* of local churches, themselves truly united, where all of the elements noted above are realized among its members. Such a vision follows the biblical account of the Council of Jerusalem (see Acts 15). It draws upon the experience of the first eight centuries when, although they were united, East and West had no central administrative structures that had jurisdiction in both.

The dialogues with the Methodists, Anglicans, and Lutherans (see *BU*, *GA*, and *GC*) have taken up questions related to bishops, collegiality, councils, infallibility, and even the papacy, pointing ways to a common future. When Catholic catechists teach about the pope, the councils, and the bishops, these dialogues need to be taken into account. For example, Catholics agree with Orthodox and Lutherans that the Church is infallible, but do not yet agree on how infallible decisions are to be made. Likewise, Anglicans can agree on the primacy in the Church and its appropriate exercise by the bishop of Rome, but there is not yet agreement on infallibility or on universal and ordinary jurisdiction. They do not feel that the pope exercised these in England before the Reformation, but rather intervened, on occasion, in support of the local bishops and the Archbishop of Canterbury, primate of England and now primate of the Anglican Communion worldwide.

The Orthodox also have specific difficulties with the papacy. Roman centralization, the claims to infallibility, and papal universal jurisdiction only developed in Catholic teaching and practice after full communion had finally ended. Therefore, understanding the Eastern point of view will be of particular importance in Catholic catechesis (see *Ox*).

The Catholic Church has experienced tremendous reforms in its means of making decisions and exercising authority under the Gospel in its long history. Only now is it gradually realizing the implications of the reforms of Vatican II, with increased lay participation, collegiality, and subsidiarity. The ecumenical implications of these reforms should be made clear to Catholic students. Likewise, it is important for Catholic students and catechists in formation to hear the views of ecumenical partners.

The Holy Father himself has indicated that the service rendered by his own papal office to the unity of the Church is an important Catholic priority, and one he is open and willing to discuss with our ecumenical partners, so as to better serve the ecumenical goal we share (see *UUS*, #95–96). Every level of Catholic life can participate in this openness of the Holy Father, in parish, school, diocese, or catechetical program. DREs serve as important links in listening to this international conversation by stimulating local discussions of Catholic service to the unity of the Church.

Formation for Catholic life should include learning from the decision-making styles and doctrine of the other churches. If catechists are training young and adult Catholics to take their appropriate responsibilities as full baptized ministers in parish and diocesan life, they will want to learn from Orthodox and Protestant fellow Christians that may have a longer history of lay leadership than has been the recent Catholic experience.

DREs will want to determine the appropriate ways of fostering this learning: through reading, experience of church meetings in other churches, inviting speakers, viewing videos, etc. All of these are means of implementing Pope John Paul II's call to celebrate the gifts we receive from one another in Christ.

CHRIST AND OUR LADY

Instruction about Christ, of course, is central to the whole catechetical program. When educators provide the historical background about the nature and divinity of Christ (see *CCC*, #466–469), it is important that students know that the divisions of 431 and 451 A.D. (which revolved around the true humanity and true divinity of Christ, and Mary as the Mother of God), have been healed, and that these issues no longer divide the Christian churches (see *OO*).

In teaching about the doctrine of God's grace in Jesus Christ, Catholics have always held the unmerited gift of God's free love in the death and resurrection of Jesus (see *CCC*, #654, #1987–97, #2001–5, #2018–20). One of the major issues of the Reformation was the difference of emphasis between the Protestant churches and the Catholic Church on the relationship of Christ's unmerited free grace, our response in faith, the role of good works (see *CCC*, #1709), human freedom (see *CCC*, #1704, #1731–39, #1743–47), and human sinfulness (see *CCC*, #406).

After thirty years of dialogue on the issue—that led Luther to post his ninety-five theses in 1517 and also to condemnations of positions thought to be held by Catholics and Lutherans by one another in the sixteenth century—in 1997 there was a *Joint Declaration on the Docrine of Justification* (see *Origins*, Vol. 28: No.8; also *JD* cf. and *BU*). The Lutheran World Federation (LWF) and the Holy See have approved this declaration. It claims agreement on this important dimension of the Church's teaching on the saving work of Christ.

The core of this brief affirmation is an agreement on the content of our common faith:

> Together we confess: By grace alone, in faith in Christ's saving work and not because of any merit on our part, we are accepted by God and receive the Holy Spirit, who renews our hearts while equipping and calling us to good works. (*JD*, #15)

This affirmation and the implications for teaching about sin, grace, merit, good works, and faith are important for instruction about Christ and his saving role. While different emphases will continue, Lutheran and Catholic catechists will need to collaborate in understanding how to teach not only their own position but also its relationship with the wider Christian community that shares this common faith (see *GDC*, #102).

Church history and polemics, which used to presume a difference of Christian teaching between Protestants and Catholics on this central issue, will need to be viewed in a different light. We will even want to question use of the label "Protestant" when referring to those with whom we now share this joint declaration.

In our merit-oriented, upwardly mobile world, where competition is more prized than giftedness, teaching the graciousness of a loving God, the goodness of an unmerited creation, and the trust entailed in Christian faith is a challenge for all our churches. The implications of the biblical teaching about grace are central for Christian spiritual formation.

During a major Lutheran anniversary in 1980, I wrote an article published in *Living Light* and *Lutheran Secondary School Quarterly*, which focused on the importance of our catechesis of grace in American culture. In it I noted how much Catholics had to learn from Lutherans about justification by grace. The editor asked to add a note that most Lutheran young people also thought that they were supposed to "earn their salvation," rather than recognize it as a free gift of grace in Jesus Christ. A clear biblical teaching on justification will be essential if we are to help young people develop a significant sense of spiritual confidence and trust, work against feelings of guilt and inadequacy, and respect the reality of sin and grace in their lives.

Our teaching of Christ, grace, sin, merit, and good works can only be enriched by a deepened understanding of our common biblical faith. The fact that we share it clearly with Lutherans—realizing the condemnations of the Council of Trent on this theme do not apply to those who sign the *JD* with Catholics—is an important component of our catechesis. In the U.S., the Evangelical Lutheran Church has approved the declaration while the Lutheran Church Missouri Synod has not.

In teaching about our Lady, it will be particularly important to take account of the hierarchy of truths (see *CCC*, #90, #284). All belief about the Most Blessed Virgin is faith about Christ and what he has done in his saving work for the Church—first among whose members is Mary, the Mother of God.

Catechists must distinguish between what is necessary for Catholics to believe and those private devotions that are so central to much of Catholic life. While the Church encourages devotions, which are private or liturgical, the Council admonishes against excess or confusion among the faithful (see *CCC*, #829, #970, #2673–9). Christian faith, on the other hand, requires belief in Mary's role as the Mother of God.

We share with Protestant, Orthodox, and Anglican Christians the belief in the role of Mary as Mother of God. These churches, however, do not share our convictions about the Immaculate Conception or the Assumption being dogmas necessary for salvation. Many believe them, as did Luther. In explaining them to Catholic students and to fellow Christian educators in other churches, it is important to note that the Immaculate Conception is about God's grace being given to Mary prior to any action of her own. Its focus is primarily on the Incarnation and on God's initiative. The Assumption is about God's commitment to all of us, recognizing Our Lady as the first fruits of our common resurrection in Christ (see *GDC*, #195–196).

There are many rich devotions in the Church, sometimes competitive and appearing to be more demonstrative than even our eucharistic liturgical life. It is important for Catholic catechesis and for communication with fellow Christians to note that it is the centrality of the faith that binds Catholics together in our understanding of Mary. Within that common faith, a wide variety of devotions— or none at all—is tolerated.

The most extensive of our dialogues and the most useful for our catechists on the ecumenical understanding of Mary is that between Lutherans and Catholics in this country, *The One Mediator, Mary and the Saints* (see *GC*). It treats the history of Marian doctrine and devotion, the

Reformation differences, and the common ground that Lutherans and Catholics can share in understanding Mary's role in the Church.

As liturgical, biblical, and eucharistic renewal deepens and catechesis helps our people differentiate between what is required in faith and what is permitted in devotion, Catholic perspectives on Mary will become a clearer witness to Gospel balance.

As we move more closer together, Catholics will not expect Orthodox and Protestant devotion to take on the same form as Catholic devotion anymore than there is devotional uniformity among Catholics worldwide. However, common focus on Christ and the unity of the Church will assist all in coming to a deeper appreciation of his mother and her role in salvation (see *NCS*, #520.21).

SUMMARY

Teaching Christian doctrine will be informed not only by Catholic ecumenical principles and the Catholic understanding of the Church, but also by the results of ecumenical dialogues on specific doctrinal issues. This must be viewed as an essential complement to catechetical programming.

The "teacher friendly" guides to the ecumenical results of bilateral and multilateral dialogues have yet to be written. In the meantime, DREs are important colleagues with parish ecumenical representatives and diocesan ecumenical officers in helping the fruits of theological conversation become for our parishes, as the Holy Father says, "a common heritage."

Among the examples of where this heritage is most important catechetically is in sacramental catechesis, as noted in Chapter 4. In teaching Scripture, the role and content of tradition, the nature of the Church and its goal of unity, leadership and authority in the Church, and Christ and Our Lady, specific examples have been noted as resource for catechetical work. DREs will play a critical role in helping their parishes provide opportunities for educational programs as new agreements emerge, or as training programs are developed on particular themes where the ecumenical resources are available and appropriate.

Creative DREs will want to work with Christian educators from partner churches on some of these themes. This will be especially important where agreements of some historic significance have been reached, like the *JD* with the Lutherans or the sacramental agreements with the Anglicans. They can find ways of celebrating these events in the parishes and of providing joint programs for catechists and adults.

The Lord has blessed us with a rich harvest of reconciliation in these agreements on core elements of the faith. DREs in this generation are privileged with the opportunity to fold these agreements into the task of handing on the faith of the ages to our people.

FOR REFLECTION

1. Which of the dialogues do you know most about? Which do you find most interesting? What surprises have you found in reading Catholic agreements with other churches? Where do you feel these dialogues offer the richest resources for catechesis?

2. How would you teach the Reformation now that we have agreements of such seriousness with Anglicans and Lutherans? What areas of your teaching will need to develop in light of these agreements? Where are you challenged to do more reading as a result of these dialogues?

3. How do you envision the Church and its unity in the next century? Have you ever talked to other Christians about the unity they hope and pray for? How does it differ from what you have learned? What other Christian traditions do you know besides the Catholic? How do these traditions and the Catholic heritage relate to the common tradition of the Gospel? What appreciation of Christ or the Scriptures have you received from other Christians? How do the dialogues give theological bases for these experiences? Where are you challenged to do more study and dialogue to enrich your life and your teaching?

6 Catechesis for Common Witness

When we were preparing the first class of deacons for their internships after two years of class and a year before ordination, we exercised great care in selecting mentors for their service component. It was important to place the candidates with ministers who had a deep faith, an articulate sense of vocation, and skill in the social ministry to which they were committed. Many were placed with sisters and priests in diocesan or parish work; however, we did want to place one or more candidates with a sister working in an ecumenical housing ministry in north Memphis. This would provide the opportunity for some members of the class to be working in the African American community with ministers who were representative of the Protestant as well as Catholic churches there.

Another placement was with a Baptist minister serving at Shelby County Penal Farm. We knew this placement would provide a good ecumenical experience for the deacon candidate, and would be a good experience that could be shared in our theological reflection group. More importantly, Rev. Bledsoe had the best reputation in town for ministering to the inmates.

This chapter should help DREs develop ecumenical approaches 1) to the "pastoral dimension of life in the Church"; 2) to "the moral teachings of the Church"; 3) to spiritual formation; 4) to their role "in the life and the mission of the parish"; and 5) to "the relationship of the parish catechetical program with the mission and policies of the diocesan Church" (*NCS*, #520.07, #520.09; #534.01; #539.09).

In many ways, DREs are called to juggle a variety of dimensions of parish catechetical leadership and linkages with the wider Church, Catholic and ecumenical. In some dioceses the ecumenical commission is supplemented by deanery committees and representatives, and Parish Ecumenical Representatives (PERs). These latter are important colleagues for the parish DREs in their role of promoting ecumenical formation within the parish.

In this chapter we will survey some areas of common witness, ecumenical dimensions to moral formation, spiritual nurture, organizing the parish for the ecumenical dimension of its mission, and collaboration and support with the diocese. While all of these areas do not neccessarily constitute a DRE's responsibilities, reflection on them will enhance the catechetical program of the parish and the contribution the DREs can make to the parish and diocesan team (see *DAPN* Chapter 5).

COMMON WITNESS AND SERVICE

Common approaches to mission were at the root of the modern ecumenical movement in the early twentieth century, as the European churches began to move out of the colonial era. Competing voices in the mission fields of the Third World were a counter witness to the Jesus Christ who preached love, harmony, and the unity of the Church.

Collaboration in preaching the Gospel is important, not only in missions overseas but also in bringing Christ to our own people, through both catechesis and outreach to the unchurched or alienated. This is why Pope John Paul II places so much emphasis on ecumenical common witness when he speaks of the "new evangelization," as we noted in the Introduction (see *CCC*, #855, *GDC*, #86a).

For many Catholics, their first experience of ecumenism has been through common service in the community, such as a CROP walk for hunger, pro-life witness, work for civil rights, and a host of other civic projects. The doctrinal dimension of common Baptism or the goal of full sacramental communion often comes only after having served with other Christians whose commitment and holiness become clear and whose devotion to Christ is no less central in their lives than that of Catholics.

DREs will want to provide experiences for catechists and students in common witness and service. Working on common ecumenical projects in the community are important components of formation for Christian service. Providing opportunities for those in Confirmation preparation service programs in an ecumenical setting, with a minister or congregation of another church, or with a neighborhood or citywide ecumenical agency, can help a whole class reflect on the uniqueness and importance of ecumenical approaches to community service (see *NCS*, #532.4021–22).

When teaching about the missionary dimension of the Gospel and the social justice witness of the Church in the community, ministers and those working in ecumenical agencies can provide helpful speakers and members of panels, demonstrating how to integrate the ecumenical dimensions of witness into parish life. In some neighborhoods, various Christian congregations reach out together to newcomers, the unchurched, and the alienated, encouraging the unaffiliated to join the Christian church closest to their own traditional roots or affinities. Providing opportunities for catechists to be knowledgeable of such programs and for young people to apprentice under such "ecumenical evangelical teams" is an important dimension of the DRE's service.

For some young people, adolescence is a time of testing and ambivalence about the Church and even about the faith. Even while young people are facing serious doubts, service in the community and close collaboration with youth ministers and more committed Christians are important supports during this period of testing. An ecumenical youth group, retreat, or service project can be important in providing a place for seeing faith in action, especially when a person may be in rebellion against the institution, language, and even family expressions of faith. Young peoples' discussion of their struggles with their various churches can give developing Catholics a more objective reflection on the Church and the difficulties they may be having with it.

There are some problems with common witness, however, especially with evangelical and Pentecostal Christians whose approach may be very different from the Catholic and other ecumenical Christian outreach. It is important, for example, to understand the challenge of proselytism, or unfair approaches to evangelism. The Catholic Church has been accused of proselytism among the Orthodox in Eastern Europe (see *Ox*) and among the poor and vulnerable in the U.S. African American community. It is important for Catholics to be sensitive to pressures we can place on other Christians in our schools and where we are a large majority.

In Latin America and other places that have had a Catholic monopoly on education and the means of social communication, the evangelism of insensitive groups causes hesitation about common witness and even the Church's commitment to ecumenism. Important dialogues with Baptists, Pentecostals, and other evangelicals have begun to clarify some of these issues in the context of religious liberty, and to lay the groundwork for common witness even with these groups. These dialogue results, along with the discussions on common witness between the

Catholic Church and the members of the WCC, are useful resources to inform our catechesis (see *DC*).

While Pentecostals and Catholics may seem most at odds over common witness, the 1998 Vatican/Pentecostal report *Evangelization, Proselytism and Common Witness* is able to say:

> Members of the Dialogue think that Pentecostals and Catholics already agree on critical points of faith. Recognition of this fact makes it possible for each of our communities to act in ways that do not impede the growth of the other. Lack of mutual recognition, however, has led at times to dismissive charges and countercharges (e.g., 'sects,' 'unbelievers,' 'syncretists,' etc.) and actions and counteractions (e.g., unilateral decisions for the good of one community, often at the expense of the other community) by members of both communities. These charges and actions have detracted from the ability of Catholics and Pentecostals to witness credibly before the world to the reconciling power of God through Jesus Christ. (Pontifical Council for Promoting Christian Unity, 97: 1–11, 1998, #70)

This may speak for only small groups of leaders, but DREs can take local initiatives to see that Catholics understand the possibilities with some evangelicals, that they are discriminating with how they speak of fellow Christians, and that they know how to reach out in charity to develop a basis on which common witness is possible.

In teaching about religious liberty, DREs need to help catechists and students be sensitive to the decisions made, in good conscience, even when they bring pain and division into the family. Not every one who decides to join another religious community is a victim of proselytism. As the *Vatican/Pentecostal* report states: "In facing conflicts, the right to

religious freedom must be seen in relationship to the
responsibility to respond to Christ's call for the unity of his
disciples. Christ calls Christians to live their freedom. At
the same time, He calls Christians to unity 'so that the
world may believe' (John 17:21)." (same text, #106)

MORAL FORMATION

The ethical dimension of the catechetical task is of particular urgency and delicacy in the contemporary American
cultural context. Both our Christian tradition of social
teaching, which touches on peace, justice, and respect for
the environment; and our teaching about personal morality, which touches on sexuality, honesty, and personal discipline, run quite contrary to the culture that surrounds us.
Some churches and some Catholics try to isolate themselves from society to preserve a Christian environment in
their formation. Others seek to find ways of preserving
their distinctive discipline and moral vision, and reaching
out to evangelize culture (see *GDC*, #85–86).

Fellow Christians are important colleagues in both the
moral formation of our people and in the common
approaches to influencing the ethics of society around us.
It will be important for DREs to enter discussions with
other Christian educators about their approaches to moral
formation in their congregations and to explore methods
of collaboration in the ethical component of catechesis.

Providing role models of holiness and moral integrity
from all Christian communities will be important components of ecumenical sharing. Many Protestants have a
great admiration for the service and witness of Catholics
like Dorothy Day and Mother Theresa. Likewise,
Catholics can be enriched by exposure to those Protestants and Orthodox who contribute to the pro-life movement, struggle for family values, and fight for civil and
human rights in the U.S. and around the world.

Differences on ethical issues, especially when they are polarizing in the public political environment, are challenging to our Christian charity and to a catechesis grounded on the fundamental unity we share in Christ. Catholics with their ecumenical partners have produced important sets of principles that can be useful in our catechesis. These have been published by both the WCC and the U.S. NCC (see *DC, BU*).

Several of the dialogues have taken on especially sensitive ethical issues. In all cases they have shown that disagreements in public policy issues are often grounded in common Christian principles that are given different emphases in different communities. The international Anglican-Roman Catholic dialogue, for example, has taken on the questions of contraception and remarriage after divorce, explaining in some detail the Christian bases out of which different applications have emerged (see *ARC 2*).

In our pro-life catechesis, it will be important to note churches, especially among the evangelicals and Orthodox, who share our concerns for the protection of life from conception to natural death, and who also have a common witness with us in the public policy area. Other churches may share our concern for the unborn and the dying, but they may have convictions about the government's role in these matters that may differ from ours.

It is important to clarify for our students and catechists the tremendous common ground we share, even when we seem to differ so dramatically in our public policy witness. Dialogues with the Reformed on human rights and abortion (see *BU*), and with the Methodists on end-of-life issues (see *GC*), are important resources in our pro-life catechesis, delineating common approaches and differences.

There are a few church divisions, however, that are rooted in ethical convictions. The historic Peace Churches—Quaker, Brethren, and Mennonite—for example, are separated from the rest of Christians because of, among other things, their conviction about a pacifist approach to Christian peacemaking. Catholics have much to learn from these churches, even when we do not see all our people called to pacifism. Pacifism has always been an option for Catholics, but commitment to peacemaking is central to the Gospel.

The existence of African American Christian churches is a witness to the moral failure of the Church to be adequately Christian and to witness to the inclusiveness of Christ's Gospel. We see now that it is a sin to enslave other people or to deny justice, equality, and friendship to others because of skin color or national origin. Slavery was a social sin, and racial discrimination is a personal sin. Catholics can learn a great deal, in the quest for racial equality and social justice, from the leaders and members of these African American churches. Some of their congregations have the most dramatic and well-developed social outreach programs in their communities. Visiting these churches and talking about how best to develop relationships with them are important parts of catechetical programs and development of ecumenical ties in the parish.

SPIRITUAL FORMATION

In addition to the catechesis of doctrine and morals, nurturing the prayer and spiritual life of catechists and students is central to the DRE's vocation. In the ecumenical sphere, DREs need to help catechists instruct Catholic people on the saints and martyrs of other traditions (see *UUS*, #82, #84). Reading appreciative biographies of people like Martin Luther, John Wesley, Dietrich Bonhoeffer, or Martin Luther King, Jr., can enrich the spiritual lives of teachers and students.

In preparation for the Jubilee in the year 2000, the Holy See is putting together a list of those who have given their lives for the faith from other Christian traditions as well as from the Catholic tradition. Inviting ecumenical educational colleagues into classes and teacher training sessions to talk about the holy ones from their traditions is an important way of nurturing the spiritual life of the Catholic catechetical community.

DREs can develop supportive spiritual relationships among the educators and leaders of other traditions. When we have questions or problems, do we have colleagues and friends in other churches that we can call to ask candid questions, to get personal spiritual support, or to find resources for our catechetical ministry? Do we provide a resource for information about Catholic life, about retreats and spirituality centers, or about educational programs for our Protestant and Orthodox colleagues (see *NCS*, #510.13)?

Part of Catholic education is helping catechists and students be grateful for the gifts already received from other traditions. We can open any Catholic hymnal and find hymns that were composed by Charles Wesley. This can be a great learning experience when a catechist points students to the Methodist Church down the street, or tells the story of the Wesley brothers and their impact on spiritual renewal in Britain and the U.S.

An Orthodox or Eastern Catholic colleague can come in to explain the icon and its role in Orthodox spirituality. This can be an enticing prelude to attendance at a Byzantine or other Eastern liturgy.

Ecumenical days of recollection and retreats, Bible study groups and prayer sessions, and common study days about a spiritual leader or ecumenical spiritual theme are all programs to which DREs can make significant contributions. Continuing ecumenical formation is essential for DREs and catechists (see *GDC*, #69–71).

Including regular ecumenical prayer intentions in parish liturgy and catechetical programs is an important dimension of spiritual nurture. Learning ecumenical dialogue as an element in Catholic spirituality is an important part of the formation process. Dialogue itself becomes both a means and a goal of spiritual formation. The Graymoor Ecumenical and Interreligious Institute provides useful material for the annual Week of Prayer for Christian Unity (see *NCS*, #510.03, #510.05, #510.07; #539.08).

STRUCTURING THE PARISH FOR ECUMENICAL MISSION

DREs reading through this book could easily be discouraged at the sheer richness of the challenges put before the Church in promoting Christian unity in the catechetical vocation. For that reason, it is important to realize that both catechesis and promoting the unity of the Church are collaborative enterprises. DREs bring their gifts, their specific calling, and their role in the parish team to this process (see *GDC*, #239).

Parish councils and parish committees have their appropriate roles to play in the service of the unity of the churches to which the Catholic congregation is called. As noted above, some dioceses mandate a Parish Ecumenical Representative in each congregation and an ecumenical coordinator in each deanery. Where this is the case, DREs can work with them to see that the proper ecumenical formation programs are provided for the catechists. The catechetical resource center should be well stocked with the right books and resources. The educational and ecumenical programs of the parish can work in strong partnership.

Where the diocese does not provide such a structure, the DRE can encourage the parish council to have someone especially devoted to following the ecumenical program of the Church and to developing the ecumenical dimension of the parish. Someone on the parish council who can provide the information and advocate for the program inherent in Catholic ecumenism can be a service to the whole parish community. Teachers or couples in ecumenical marriages can be significant candidates for such a role.

Dioceses and parishes need to be as serious about the formation opportunities for volunteer ecumenists and catechists in the parish as they are about those called to education in the secular subjects in Catholic schools (see *GDC*, #73). Parish liturgy committees, education boards, social outreach programs, and ministry coordinating groups will be well served by appointing one member to be particularly attentive to the ecumenical dimension of that aspect of parish work, and to be in touch with other Christian partners in the community working on the same dimension of church life in their congregations.

The priests in the parish have a particular role in ecumenical leadership, depending on their gifts and interests. However, ecumenical direction should not fall solely to the rectory. Interchurch families need to be integrated into regular parish life and have opportunities for leadership provided that will build on their potential for ecumenical leadership and witness (see *NCS*, #531.041–.043; #532.2031–.32; #539.07).

Joint meetings of parish staff and representatives of other congregations are important. These groups can share analyses of the Christian needs and situations of the local communities, plan common approaches to education and community outreach, and listen to current developments coming from the wider Church (see *GDC*, #279–280). Building the local community into an experience of itself as the People of God that is welcoming and hospitable for all entails ecumenical sensitivity and planning. The local Christian community centered on the parish can include the other Christian congregations in the neighborhood as parts of its sense of community and missional life (see *NCS*, #532.201–.202).

For example, as a community prepares for Jubilee 2000, parish staffs from several neighborhood congregations can share what they are planning within their own communities, what is going on with their church nationally and internationally, what resources are available, and what can be done locally to provide joint projects and celebrations. As the *JD* becomes a priority, two congregations can decide together how to celebrate the fact. They can provide common catechesis and discussion so that the declaration becomes part of parish life. In fact, they can work together to implement or study any national or synod/diocesan initiatives.

DREs have to be careful not to take on too many parish responsibilities, even in the educational area. However, they can facilitate the collaborative approach that brings new leaders into ministry and empowers these leaders with the knowledge and support that can sustain them. DREs can continue to encourage and challenge these people to take on the ecumenical responsibility that will facilitate the whole parish. Many DRE skills are the same as those that will serve people in ecumenical ministry as well.

DIOCESAN SUPPORT AND COLLABORATION

DREs are usually well supported by the diocesan religious education/catechetical office and other elements of the diocesan pastoral center. Also, each diocese should have an ecumenical officer and an ecumenical commission. Many dioceses belong to local and state councils of churches and have ongoing dialogues with specific church communities in the diocese. Seminaries or Catholic colleges within the diocese may provide programs and resources for ecumenical ministry training programs and catechist formation.

"The Bishops may deem opportune or necessary specific ecumenical cooperation in the area of religious instruction" (*GDC*, #198).

Collaboration with all these structures is an important contribution from the Catholic educational community to the common diocesan and ecumenical enterprise. The ecumenical officer should be a useful resource for information, materials, and contacts for DREs. The diocesan ecumenical guidelines, the results of diocesan and national dialogues, and specific relationships like covenants are important content that DREs can use in their catechesis and teacher enrichment (see *GDC*, #265 ff.).

The Catholic educational community needs to be taken into account when constructing a diocesan ecumenical commission or providing a Catholic delegation to represent the Church on boards of state and city councils of churches. The religious educators of the diocese should be represented around the table in discussions of the ecumenical program of the diocese. DREs and catechists should be available for such commission or board service. They can help the diocesan ecumenical officer in surfacing names that can well represent the Catholic educational community in ecumenical service.

While the *GDC* talks about developing catechetical material for the local church, this is difficult in the U.S. We have large publishing companies that provide fine materials for use all over the country. For this reason, the culture, ecumenical context, and priorities of the local diocesan church are not able to be incorporated into the published catechetical material. Therefore, DREs and ecumenical officers will need to collaborate with others in providing the appropriate programming and resources to inculturate and adapt catechetical material for local needs (see *GDC*, #131–136, #213–214, #217 ff.).

In many dioceses around the country, the ecumenical offices have emerged from the Catholic educational community. Some dioceses have written ecumenical educational programming, often with other churches, that has been an important national as well as diocesan contribution. The diocesan ecumenical office can often be helpful to the DRE in finding ecumenically adept educators who can serve in diocesan or parish ecumenical leadership.

Unity within the Catholic Church as well as between Catholics and fellow Christians is an important dimension of the DRE's mission. When searching for people for ecumenical leadership, it is important that all ideological elements in the parish and diocese be involved.

When we put together the Presbyterian-Catholic task force in Memphis, we included one interchurch couple. The Presbyterian wife in that couple was much more sympathetic to the Catholic Church and its conciliar renewal than was her Catholic husband, who designated himself a "pre-Trent" Catholic. He brought not only credibility to the task force, but honestly raised many of the hard questions that Catholics in the pews would bring to their Presbyterian partners and to ecumenically attuned Catholics.

The ecumenical work needs to focus on the parish and congregation. However, the resources of the diocese—and the parish contribution to its program—are important dimensions of our educational and ecumenical work. A spirit of collaboration, mutual support, and occasional challenge will enhance the Spirit's work at every level of church life and in each dimension of our responsibility (see *NCS*, #510.10).

SUMMARY

Catechesis for mission is an essential element of a DRE's calling. Common witness and service in the community, and an ecumenical dimension to the moral formation and spiritual nurture of the people, are essential to a Catholic understanding of our mission today. In carrying out their component of this mission, DREs help catechists to collaborate with the parish staff and local ecumenical colleagues, and to work with diocesan program colleagues in enabling the ecumenical and educational task of the local church.

While the word "ecumenical" means universal, worldwide, or global, the unity it represents among Christians can only be realized by local educational programming, relationships, and building up Christ's will for the Church. This is done through spiritual, intellectual, experiential, and behavioral nurture in each place around the globe where the People of God collaborate to be faithful to the Gospel. DREs have an important role in nurturing this sense of mission and these strategies of solidarity in each local situation.

FOR REFLECTION

1. Where have you experienced Christians working together in service to the world or in witness to the Gospel? What needs in your community could be met more effectively by sharing a common Christian commitment among the churches? What agencies provide support for churches working together in your neighborhood or state?

2. Where is the spirituality of unity being cultivated in your catechetical program? What ideas do you have for deepening the ecumenical spiritual life of your parish? What are the moral issues in your community on which the churches collaborate? Where are there tensions on ethical issues? What ideas do you have for bringing reconciliation to these tensions?

3. Who assumes ecumenical responsibility in your parish? How does the religious education program of the parish support the congregation's work for unity? What more can be done? Do you know a contact person in the ecumenical office of the diocese and the program of the commission? Where can you best contribute to the parish and diocesan programs?

Conclusion

When I began teaching in 1959 at St. George's in Evanston, Illinois, I was criticized for teaching my freshman religion class that they might possibly celebrate Mass in their own language some day. I responded to that criticism (in a rather unpolitic way!) by telling my students that they could find Mass being celebrated in the vernacular, Arabic, and occasionally English a mere three stops down on the "El," at St. George's Melkite Church. I also told them that they could receive Communion in the Body and Blood of Christ—and that they should! Of course we did, eventually, take them down for just such a celebration.

I used to wonder if my students, as a result of these experiences, were better prepared for the coming of the good Pope John XXIII's Second Vatican Council and its renewal of our liturgical life. Now, of course, few catechists remember those days before the conciliar reforms, when Latin prevailed and we taught that it was not possible for the Church to change its form of worship.

Should not students come away from their catechetical formation with an impatience for the unity of the Church and the skills and knowledge necessary for deepening the bonds of our parishes, dioceses, and churches as they seek to realize God's will? Should they not be preparing to live, work, and pray with fellow Christians—with whom they already share more than divides them?

Pope John Paul II continually reminds us that we share more with fellow Christians than divides us. He was most clear in speaking to Episcopal and Catholic bishops regarding the ordination of women in the Anglican Communion: we should not be surprised nor deterred from the goal of full communion by new challenges we face, like differences over the ordination of women. If we can light a fire among our young people that lets them love the Church and its sacraments and inspires them to deepen our common life with other fellow Christians, have we not made a great contribution, as catechists, to what the Spirit is doing in the world?

The *GDC* challenges us:

> Every Christian community, by the mere fact of being what it is, is moved by the Spirit to recognize its ecumenical vocation in the circumstances in which it finds itself, by participating in ecumenical dialogue and initiatives to foster the unity of Christians.
>
> Catechesis, therefore, is always called to assume an 'ecumenical dimension' (*Catechesi tradendae*, #32) everywhere.
>
> • This is done, firstly, by an exposition of all of Revelation. . . .
>
> • In the second place, . . . catechesis brings to the fore that unity of faith which exists . . . explains divisions. . . . and the steps being taken to overcome them (cf. *DAPN*, #190) . . . [it] also arouses and nourishes a true desire for unity . . .
>
> • Finally, . . . it prepares children, young people and adults to live in contact with brothers and

sisters of other confessions. (*GDC*, #197)

DREs have the unique role of supporting the vocation to unity of the parish, diocese, and universal Church. They also help their students and catechists come to conversion, participate in the pilgrimage, and learn the rich results of our encounters with other Christians. Unity is an affirmation all Catholic Christians make, but the experiences, the knowledge, and the action in the community implicit in this affirmation can only come about by diligent educational pursuit.

As Pope John Paul II affirms for all of us: "Concern for restoring unity pertains to the whole church, faithful and clergy alike. It extends to everyone, according to the ability of each, whether it be exercised in daily Christian living or in theological and historical studies" (*UUS*, #19). DREs have a significant contribution to make to this pilgrimage, which is the calling of the whole People of God.

Bibliography

WORKS CITED

Baptism, Eucharist and Ministry. Geneva, Switzerland: World Council of Churches, 1983.

Best, Thomas F. and Günther Gassman, eds. *On the Way to Fuller Koinonia*. Geneva, Switzerland: World Council of Churches, 1994.

Congregation for the Clergy. *General Directory for Catechesis*. Washington, DC: United States Catholic Conference, 1997.

Documentary History of Faith and Order: 1963–1993. Geneva, Switzerland: World Council of Churches, 1994.

International Commission on English in the Liturgy. *Rite of Christian Initiation of Adults*. Chicago: Liturgy Training Publications, 1988.

Joint Declaration on the Doctrine of Justification (Lutheran-Catholic). 1997.

Kinnamon, Michael and Brian E. Cope, eds. *The Ecumenical Movement: An Anthology of Basic Texts and Voices*. Grand Rapids, MI: William B. Eerdmans, 1997.

National Certification Standards for Professional Parish Directors of Religious Education. Washington, DC: National Conference for Catechetical Leadership, 1996.

Pontifical Council for Promoting Christian Unity. *Directory for the Application of Principles and Norms on Ecumenism*. Washington, DC: United States Catholic Conference, 1995.

_____. *Evangelization, Proselytism and Common Witness*. 1998.

Pope John Paul II. *Ut Unum Sint (That They May Be One)*. 1995.

Second Vatican Council. *Unitatis redintegratio (Decree on Ecumenism)*. 1964. From Flannery, Austin, O.P., ed. *Vatican Council II, Volume I, Revised Edition: The Conciliar and Post Conciliar Documents*. Northport, NY: Costello Publishing Company, 1998.

Secretariat for Ecumenical and Interreligious Affairs, ed. *Ecumenical Formation of Pastoral Workers*. Washington, DC: United States Catholic Conference, 1998.

FOR FURTHER READING

Brown, Raymond, et al. *Mary in the New Testament: A Collaborative Assessment by Protestant and Roman Catholic Scholars.* Minneapolis: Augsburg Fortress Publishers, 1978.

———. *Peter in the New Testament.* New York: Paulist Press, 1973.

Campbell, Ted. *Christian Confessions: A Historical Introduction.* Louisville: Westminster/John Knox, 1996.

Casarella, Peter and Raúl Gómez. *El Cuerpo de Cristo: The Hispanic Presence in the U.S. Catholic Church.* New York: Crossroads Publishing, 1998.

Fey, Harold, ed. *The Ecumenical Advance: A History of the Ecumenical Movement 1948–1968.* Geneva, Switzerland: World Council of Churches, 1986.

Ford, John T. and Darlis J. Swan. *Twelve Tales Untold: A Study Guide for Ecumenical Reception.* Grand Rapids, MI: William B. Eerdmans, 1993.

Groupe des Dombes. *For the Conversion of the Churches.* Geneva, Switzerland: World Council of Churches, 1993.

Lossky, Nicholas, et al., eds. *Dictionary of the Ecumenical Movement.* Grand Rapids, MI: William B. Eerdmans, 1991.

Oakham, Ronald A. *One at the Table: The Reception of Baptized Christians.* Chicago: Liturgy Training Publications, 1996.

Renew 2000. *Ecumenical Handbook.* 1232 George Street, Plainfield, NJ, 07062.

Riggs, Ann, Eamon McManus and Jeffrey Gros. *Introduction to Ecumenism.* New York: Paulist Press, 1998.

Roman Catholic-Presbyterian/Reformed Consultation. *Laity in the Church and in the World: Resources for Ecumenical Dialogue.* Washington, DC: United States Catholic Conference, 1998.

Rouse, Ruth and Stephen Neill, eds. *History of the Ecumenical Movement 1517–1948.* London: Society for the Promotion of Christian Knowledge, 1954.

Shriver, Peggy. *Having Gifts That Differ: Profiles of Ecumenical Churches.* New York: Friendship Press, 1990.

United Methodist-Catholic Dialogue. *Yearning for Unity: Small Group Parish Study Resources.* Washington, DC: United States Catholic Conference, 2000.

Watley, William. *Singing the Lord's Song in a Strange Land: The African-American Churches and Ecumenism.* Lawrenceville, NJ: Africa World Press, 1993.

Resources

Graymoor Ecumenical and Interreligious Institute
475 Riverside Dr., #1960
New York, New York 10115
212-870-2332
(*Ecumenical Trends*, Week of Prayer for Christian Unity)

Canadian Centre for Ecumenism
2065 Sherbrooke St. W.
Montreal, QC, H3H 1G6
Canada
514-937-9176
(*Ecumenism*)

National Association of Diocesan Ecumenical Officers
4177 Marlborough Avenue
San Diego, California 92105
(*Newsletter*)
http://www.peppercornplace.com/~nadeo/news.htm

National Association of Evangelicals
450 Gundersen Drive
Carol Stream, Illinois 60188
630-665-0500

The National Council of Churches
475 Riverside Drive
New York, New York 10027
212-870-2141

Secretariat for Ecumenical and Interreligious Affairs
National Conference of Catholic Bishops
3211 4th St. NE
Washington, D.C. 20017
202-541-3020

World Council of Churches (New York office)
475 Riverside Dr.
New York, New York 10027
212-870-3193
(book order 800-523-8211)